JULY 2019

Tell Me How This Ends

Military Advice, Strategic Goals, and the "Forever War" in Afghanistan

AUTHOR
Mark F. Cancian

A Report of the CSIS International Security Program

CSIS | CENTER FOR STRATEGIC & INTERNATIONAL STUDIES

ROWMAN & LITTLEFIELD
Lanham • Boulder • New York • London

About CSIS

Established in Washington, D.C., over 50 years ago, the Center for Strategic and International Studies (CSIS) is a bipartisan, nonprofit policy research organization dedicated to providing strategic insights and policy solutions to help decisionmakers chart a course toward a better world.

In late 2015, Thomas J. Pritzker was named chairman of the CSIS Board of Trustees. Mr. Pritzker succeeded former U.S. senator Sam Nunn (D-GA), who chaired the CSIS Board of Trustees from 1999 to 2015. CSIS is led by John J. Hamre, who has served as president and chief executive officer since 2000.

Founded in 1962 by David M. Abshire and Admiral Arleigh Burke, CSIS is one of the world's preeminent international policy institutions focused on defense and security; regional study; and transnational challenges ranging from energy and trade to global development and economic integration. For eight consecutive years, CSIS has been named the world's number one think tank for defense and national security by the University of Pennsylvania's "Go To Think Tank Index."

The Center's over 220 full-time staff and large network of affiliated scholars conduct research and analysis and develop policy initiatives that look to the future and anticipate change. CSIS is regularly called upon by Congress, the executive branch, the media, and others to explain the day's events and offer bipartisan recommendations to improve U.S. strategy.

CSIS does not take specific policy positions; accordingly, all views expressed herein should be understood to be solely those of the author(s).

ISBN: 978-1-4422-8125-7 (pb); 978-1-4422-8126-4 (eBook)

Center for Strategic & International Studies
1616 Rhode Island Avenue, NW
Washington, D.C. 20036
202-887-0200 | www.csis.org

Roman & Littlefield
4501 Forbes Boulevard
Lanham, MD 20706
301-459-3366 | www.roman.com

Acknowledgments

This report is funded by a grant from the Koch Foundation.

The author would like to thank James Meil for his research support throughout the course of this study.

Finally, the author thanks the many interviewees, working group members, and reviewers—inside CSIS and outside—who answered questions, read the draft, and provided valuable comments. Their contributions improved the final report, but the content presented here, including any errors, remains solely the responsibility of the author.

Contents

Executive Summary

When the United States invaded Afghanistan after the attacks on September 11, 2001, and overthrew the Taliban regime, senior military officers were not predicting that the United States would remain militarily involved 18 years later. However, after expending nearly $800 billion and suffering 2,400 killed, the United States is still there, having achieved a stalemate at best.

One key element at the root of this frustration has been the inability of successive administrations to recognize that their nation-building goals require a long and intense commitment of forces and resources. The initial narrow focus on counterterrorism against Al Qaeda limited the ambitions and commitment of the U.S. in the region. However, between 2002 and 2004, U.S. goals expanded to include a fundamental transformation of Afghan society, politics, and culture—in other words, nation-building.

This expansion of goals was a choice. And yet, there is no evidence that the connection between the desired end states and the efforts required to achieve them was ever discussed at the highest levels. Although this was a failing of both civilian and military officials, the consequences fell mostly on the military: despite their need to estimate force requirements, defend them publicly, and then attain the goals on the ground. This lack of discussion—and the military's unwillingness or inability to make the goals-effort connection—allowed the United States to drift into a long, costly, and thus far indecisive conflict.

What does nation-building in Afghanistan entail? It seeks to create the Western vision of a modern nation: a state with a strong central government, the impartial rule of law, political leadership chosen through democratic processes, religious differences tolerated, speech uncensored, a market economy operating, human rights respected, and women and girls empowered.

Nation-building is not bad. It promotes—or imposes, depending on one's perspective—values that modern states believe are important. However, even if successful, it is a multigenerational effort. Nation-building in Afghanistan is particularly challenging because it requires profound changes to Afghan political and social life. It proposes to take a society that is politically decentralized, religiously devout, socially conservative, clan and tribe based, and patriarchal, and to turn it into the Western vision of a twenty-first-century society. The U.S.-led coalition is endeavoring to change an Afghan's relationship with his family, his government, and his God.

The George W. Bush administration's expanded goals were a classic case of "mission creep," so often warned about after the tragic events in Somalia in 1993 when a humanitarian operation degenerated into combat against local warlords. The problem is not that the mission crept—such a change may well have been prudent—but that it crept stealthily, without debate.

When the Obama administration began its surge in Afghanistan, it focused its rhetoric on Al Qaeda but was unable to give up on nation-building goals. As a result, the administration got caught between its intent to limit the time and resources committed to the surge and the advice coming from the military leadership, which insisted that the required counterinsurgency campaign would need more forces and more time. This dichotomy poisoned civil-military relations for the entirety of the Obama administration.

The expanded mission of nation-building in Afghanistan, as well as growing insurgency in the region, put senior military officers in a difficult position. They repeatedly stated that the conflict would be long and asked for more troops, although they did not foresee the two-decade-long commitment that ensued. Yet, they also expressed confidence—often parodied in satirical veteran websites—that the campaign was making progress, even as the situation on the ground got worse. Although these statements did spark conversations about how many troops should be deployed, there was no discussion about the relationship between the desired end state and the military effort required to reach it, nor did the military leadership push for such a discussion.

The United States military's inability to accurately estimate the length and intensity of the conflict in Afghanistan occurred for many reasons, but a significant contribution came from the hubris of being a militarily dominant superpower. This showed in several ways:

- Ignoring that other nations might not have the same values that we do;
- Ignoring the experience of the Soviets, who—despite obvious differences to the U.S. coalition—had tried to achieve many of the same social and political transformations, and who had experienced many of the same frustrations that the U.S. and NATO later experienced;
- Ignoring the history of foreign occupations in general, which inevitably engender resentment against the foreign occupier;
- Ignoring the history of Afghanistan, which had a precedent of being easy to conquer but difficult to occupy; and
- Ignoring why the Taliban fight, particularly their religious motivation.

Military advice was also constrained by a belief that the military should not participate in discussions about goals and end states at all: many military officers are uncomfortable with the political dimensions of these discussions and prefer to focus on implementation, thus separating the civilian and military spheres. At the highest levels, however, such a separation is not possible, because the two spheres are intertwined. Thus, this paper argues that the military should participate in strategic discussions of this nature, even if the ultimate decision rests with the president and civilian officials.

The purpose in offering recommendations is to help create conditions for the United States to go into conflicts with its eyes wide open when it faces such decisions in the future; that is, for it to understand that choices about end states entail commitments of a given potential length and intensity. The military in particular needs to make this connection between ends and effort, since it is tasked with implementing the course of action that is chosen. Consequently, the project presented in this report recommends the following:

- Creating a dialogue between senior military and civilian officials to discuss the relationship between goals/end state of a military effort and its intensity/duration;
- Requiring more clarity from civilian officials in early stages of conflict by updating the way in which Authorization for the Use of Military Force (AUMF) documents are constructed and legislated;
- Continuing to develop military strategists and ensuring that they are credible to warfighters;
- Taking the history and experience of others seriously;
- Revising publications on military doctrine to include discussion of choices about goals end states

1 | Introduction

18 Years of Unexpected War

*"KABUL – A Command Sergeant Major serving in Kabul who reportedly said he'd fight the war 'so his son wouldn't have to' in 2001 feels like an ***hole right now, after his son joined the Army a year ago and now serves with a unit just a few miles away. 'When I said that, I thought we were going to come in, bomb the shit out of them, shoot a few guys, and split,' said Sgt. Maj. Ted Stevens while noting previous U.S. engagements without a prolonged troop presence such as Vietnam and Korea."*

– Duffel Blog

A paradox drove this research project. When the United States invaded Afghanistan after the attacks on September 11, 2001, and subsequently overthrew the Taliban regime, senior military officials were not predicting that the United States would still be militarily involved 18 years later. Yet, here we are.

Indeed, the unexpectedly long U.S. involvement has become the stuff of ridicule, appearing regularly in *Duffel Blog*, a military satire website.[1]

The current project seeks to understand how this happened. It focuses on one element: military advice about the duration and intensity of the conflict. Military advice is not the only element that has shaped U.S. involvement, but it is one that has not received much attention; crucially, understanding why the military leadership failed to advise civilian decisionmakers about the military implications of their goals will be instrumental in avoiding such frustrating conflicts in the future.

The purpose of this project is not to indicate how to fight such wars better in the future. Rather, its goal is to aid in developing more insightful advice before wars begin, so that the United States can determine whether to get involved in the first place—and understand the likely duration and intensity of the commitment if it does. As Lieutenant General Daniel Bolger observed: "With minimal domestic debate—and, notably, no known military objection—the administration backed into two lengthy, indecisive counterinsurgency campaigns, Afghanistan under-resourced, and Iraq overly optimistic. The limited ends of containing Islamist movements and attriting Al Qaeda faded into the background, at least until Sunni Arabs and a resurgent Taliban made it

1. The example in the text box comes from *Duffel Blog*, January 13, 2014

obvious that neither Iraq nor Afghanistan seem likely to move readily into the orbit of Western democratic republics."[2]

Developing a consensus about ends, ways, and means at the beginning of the conflict will also ease some of the civil-military tensions that arose during the war due to the fact that the civilian leadership was unwilling to stay for generations but also unwilling to give up its extensive nation-building goals. The military found itself struggling to implement this inconsistent strategy, asking for increased resources and more time that the civilian leadership was willing to grant.

This report, the culmination of a six-month research project, is organized as follows:

Chapter 2 documents the high stakes involved. Although the intensity of the Afghanistan conflict is down from its peak, the war continues, the cost is substantial, and the current state of affairs is at best a stalemate.

Chapter 3 analyzes how the desired goals and end states for the conflict drive the military effort in Afghanistan.[3] It describes how U.S. goals were initially limited, but that they expanded in 2004 to a broad nation-building agenda, which has continued ever since, although there may have been a recent shift as negotiations with the Taliban have stepped up. It further describes why the 2004 expansion is a classic case of mission creep and why nation-building, though sometimes successful, is a multigenerational effort.

Chapter 4 documents how the ambitious nation-building end state drove senior military officers to give particular advice about the length of the war, defined their statements of progress, and motivated their continuous requests for more troops.

Chapter 5 looks at why there was no military warning of likely consequences ahead of this mission expansion. In particular, it examines the hubris of a superpower that thought it could ignore previous experience.

Chapter 6 answers the question of whether the military should offer strategic advice about goals and end states. One reason the military did not warn about the duration and intensity of the conflict was that some commentators and military officers would limit the military's role to the implementation of goals specified by civilian authorities. This chapter argues that ends and means are so intertwined at the highest decision-making levels that military officials must participate fully in strategy development.

Finally, Chapter 7 provides recommendations for future military officers to provide insightful advice to civilian officials. With this insight, authorities will be able to know what they are getting into when faced with similar situations in the future, allowing them not to blunder into open-ended, inconclusively stable campaigns.

---

2. Lieutenant General Daniel P. Bolger, *Why We Lost: A General's Inside Account of the Iraq and Afghanistan Wars* (New York: Houghton Mifflin Harcourt, 2014), 422.
3. This study uses "goals" and "end state" as synonyms. However, as military terminology is evolving, "end state" is losing favor because it suggests a stop to the unending flow of history. "Goals," on the other hand, does not imply this permanent condition. Nevertheless, because "end state" has been used so frequently in the last several decades and continues to be used in military doctrine, it is used here. JP 1-02 Dictionary of Military and Associated Terms contains the following definition: "end state—The set of required conditions that defines achievement of the commander's objectives." Military doctrinal manuals also use "objective" is a synonym for "goals."

2 | Why It Matters

High Costs and Unsatisfactory Outcome

Protracted conflicts like the one in Afghanistan do not cripple superpowers. As a percentage of gross domestic product, the fiscal cost is low; the human cost, while tragic, is far less than what was seen during the wars in Vietnam and Korea. Nevertheless, the war exacts a price from Americans. The fiscal costs constrain what can be done domestically and add to an already excessive national debt. The high level of troop deployments stresses the force and diverts attention from other international engagements. Finally, prolonged conflicts are not a U.S. strength, as public support erodes over time and the conflicts become a political problem for the administration in power.

Down from Peak Intensity but Still Going

Measured by troop strength, U.S. engagement in Afghanistan is far down from the 2010/2011 peak during the surge, but the troop level still runs to about 15,000, a number, which has crept up as the Trump administration reacted to Taliban successes on the battlefield. These levels will likely to remain stable for the foreseeable future, as there are currently no plans for reductions or withdrawal.

Figure 1: U.S. Troop Level in Afghanistan 2001–2019

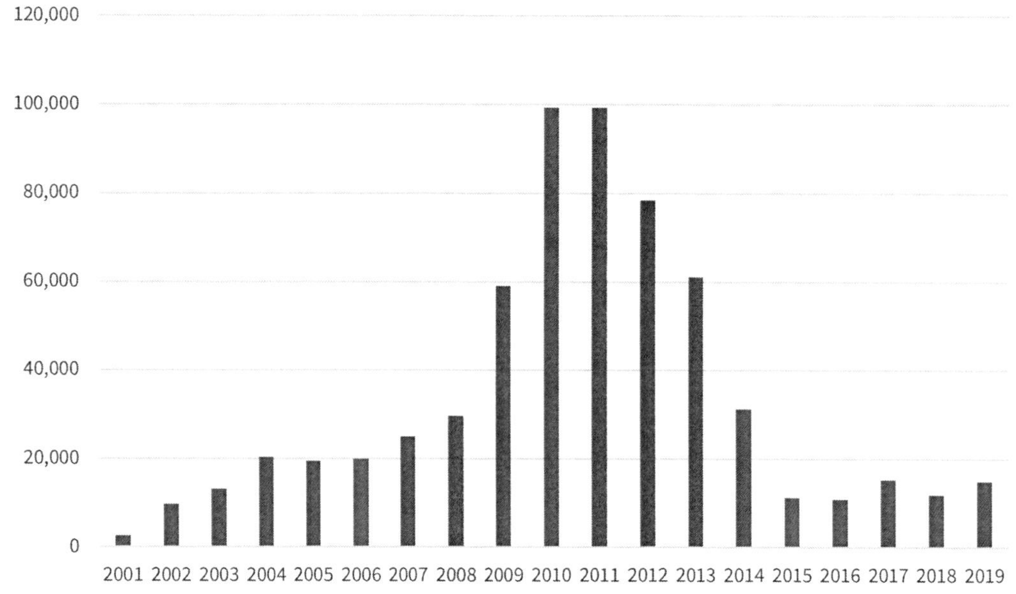

Source: Defense Manpower Data Center; DOD FY 2020 Budget Overview[4]

Measuring the war's fiscal cost shows the same cycle, with expenses down from their peak during the surge but still substantial. Total military costs for the war in Afghanistan through 2019 are $737 billion, with another $44 billion in State Department costs. Further, many more expenses, such as those related to medical care for veterans and repair of worn equipment, are expected to occur in the future.[5]

4. Department of Defense, Defense Manpower Data Center, *DoD Personnel, Workforce Reports, and Publications* (Sep. 2009-Sep.2017), accessed May 13, 2019, https://www.dmdc.osd.mil/appj/dwp/dwp_reports.jsp;Office of the Undersecretary of Defense (Comptroller)/Chief Financial Officer, *Defense Budget Overview: United States Department of Defense Fiscal Year 2020 Budget Request* (DOD, 2019), https://comptroller.defense.gov/Portals/45/Documents/defbudget/fy2020/fy2020_Budget_Request_Overview_Book.pdf.
5. For an example that includes many more costs than the DoD tabulation, see: Joseph E. Stiglitz and Linda J. Bilmes, *The $3 Trillion War* (WW Norton and Company, 2009).

Figure 2: Fiscal Cost of Afghan War 2001–2019

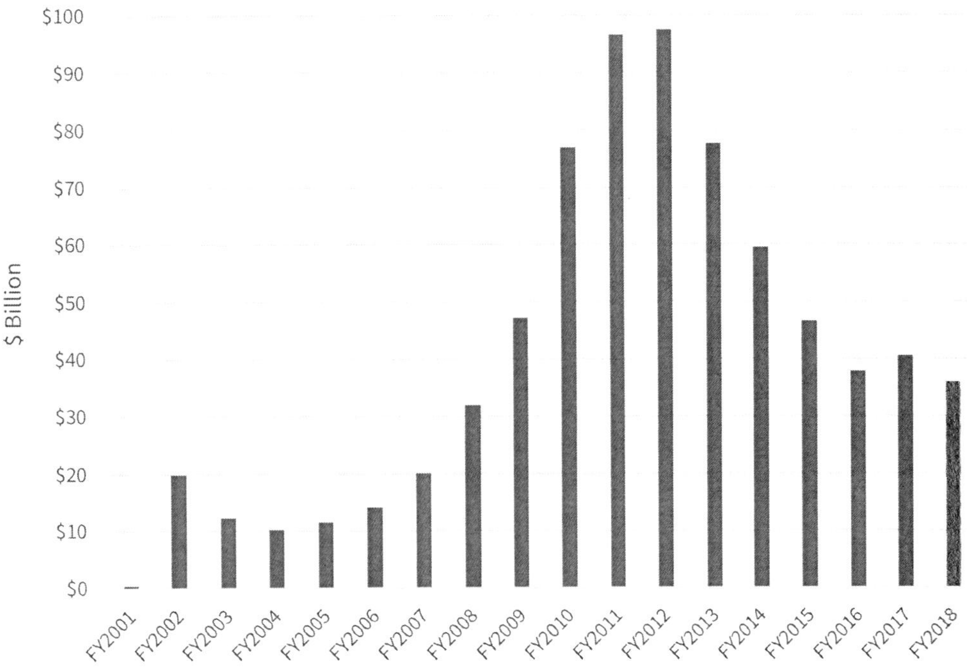

Source: Department of Defense6; estimated costs for Afghanistan include related regional costs that support combat operations in the U.S. Central Command area of responsibility.

In addition to fiscal costs, there are human costs. 2,418 U.S. service members have lost their lives in Afghanistan to date (total killed from both hostile and nonhostile causes), although those losses have fortunately eased off in recent years as U.S. forces have moved towards advising and assisting roles.[7] Casualties among Afghan security forces and civilians have remained high, however, with over 34,000 civilians killed since the beginning of the conflict.[8]

Measured by the number of munitions dropped, the war is intensifying. This reflects the fact that as the conflict continues, it is principally being borne on the ground by Afghan security forces. It may also reflect the strengthening insurgency as coalition forces have withdrawn.

---

6. U.S. Department of Defense, *Cost of War Update Through March 2018*, https://fas.org/man/eprint/cow/fy2018q2.pdf; Congressional Research Service, *US War Costs, Casualties, and Personnel Levels since 9/11*, April 18, 2019, https://fas.org/sgp/crs/natsec/IF11182.pdf.
7. "U.S. Military Casualties - Operation Enduring Freedom (OEF) and Operation Freedom's Sentinel (OFS)," *Defense Casualty Analysis System*, June 17, 2019, https://dcas.dmdc.osd.mil/dcas/pages/casualties.xhtml.
8. United Nations Assistance Mission in Afghanistan, *Afghanistan: Protection of Civilians in Armed Conflict Annual Report 2018* (UNAMA, 2019), https://unama.unmissions.org/sites/default/files/unama_annual_protection_of_civilians_report_2018_-_23_feb_2019_-_english.pdf; Marc E. Garlasco, *"Troops in Contact": Airstrikes and Civilian Deaths in Afghanistan* (New York: Human Rights Watch, 2008), https://www.hrw.org/reports/2008/afghanistan0908/1.htm#_Toc208224416.

Figure 3: Munitions Dropped in Afghanistan 2004–2018

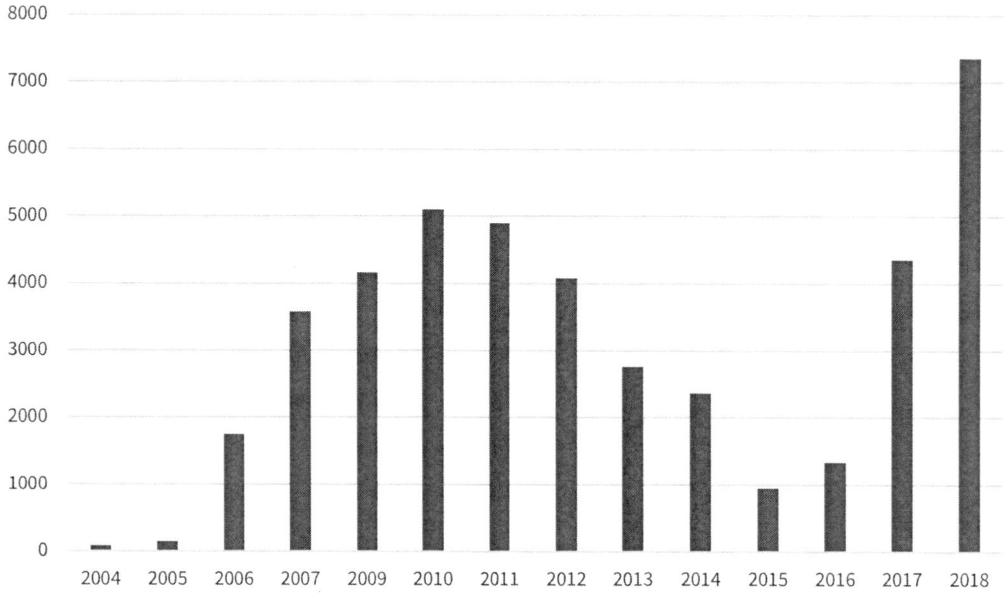

Source: U.S. Air Forces Central Command[9]; 2008 data not available

After 18 Years a Stalemate . . . at Best

Most assessments of the current state of the war in Afghanistan call it a stalemate, with momentum possibly moving against the Kabul government. The chart below shows changes in security assessments over time. Despite intense efforts by the coalition, security has essentially remained unchanged for the last three years, hence the notion of stalemate.

9. U.S. Air Forces Central Command Public Affairs, "Combined Forces Air Component Commander Air Power Statistics," U.S. Air Forces Central Command, accessed May 14, 2019, https://www.afcent.af.mil/About/Airpower-Summaries/.

Figure 4: Security in Afghanistan 2016–2018

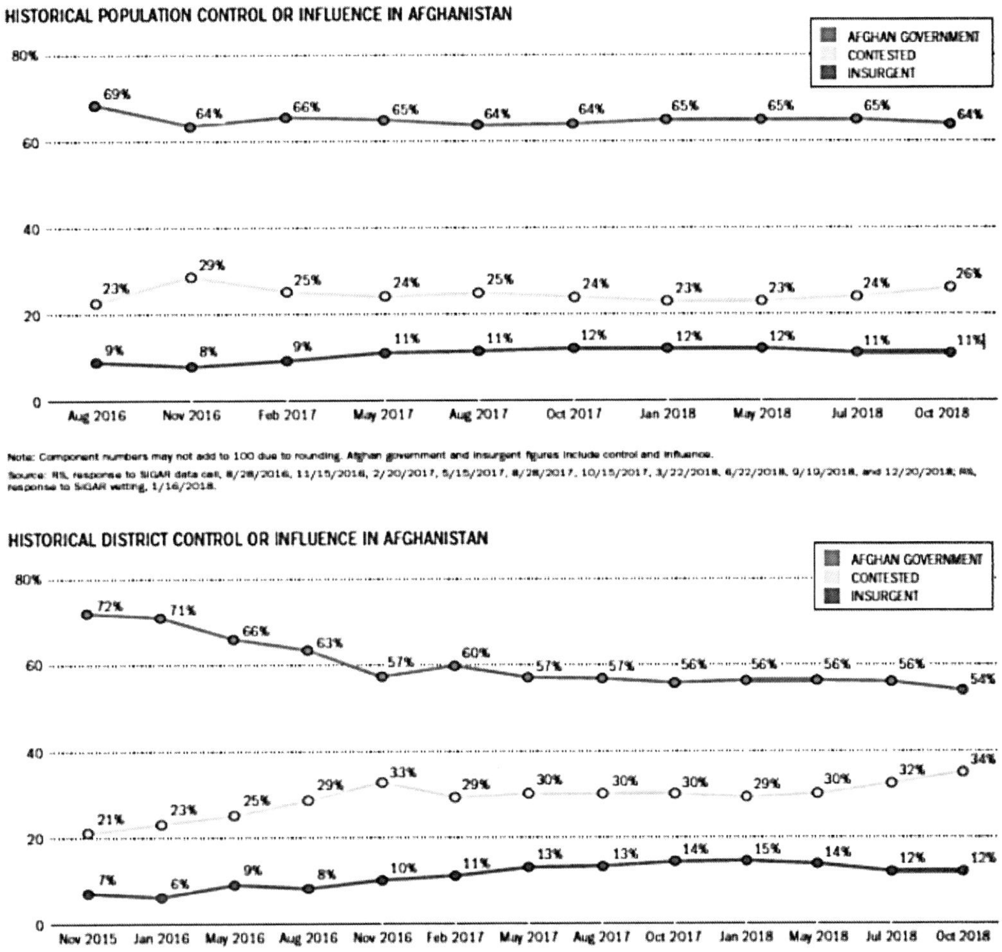

Source: Anthony Cordesman, A War in Crisis! Afghanistan in Mid-2019[10]

Currently, the coalition assesses that the Kabul government controls or influences 54 percent of the districts and 63 percent of the population. The Kabul government is stronger in the population centers and weaker in the countryside.

Table 1: Level of Security in Afghanistan, Government Estimate, 2019

	Districts (%)	Population (%)
Kabul government controlled	54	63
Taliban controlled	12	11
Contested	34	26

Source: Special Inspector General for Afghanistan Reconstruction[11]

10. Anthony Cordesman, *A War in Crisis! Afghanistan in Mid-2019* (Washington DC: CSIS, 2019), https://www.csis.org/analysis/war-crisis-afghanistan-mid-2019.
11. Special Inspector General for Afghanistan Reconstruction, *SIGAR Quarterly Report to the United States Congress*, (Arlington, VA, January 2019), https://www.sigar.mil/pdf/quarterlyreports/2019-01-30qr.pdf ; Lead Inspector General, *Operation Freedom's Sentinel: Lead Inspector General Report to the U.S. Congress October 1, 2018 to December 31, 2018*, 18. https://www.dodig.mil/in-the-Spotlight/Article/1761207/lead-inspector-general-for-operation-free-

However, independent experts Bill Roggio and Alexandra Gutowski at the Long War Journal provide a more pessimistic assessment of the situation. Based on a close reading of publicly available information they show much more of the country as "contested" than does the coalition assessment (42 percent versus 26 percent of the population).

Table 2: Current Level of Security in Afghanistan, Independent Estimate

	Districts (%)	Population (%)
Kabul government controlled	35	49
Taliban controlled	13	9
Contested	52	42

Source: The Long War Journal[12]

They conclude: "[S]ince the U.S. drawdown of peak forces in 2011, the Taliban has unquestionably been resurgent."[13]

Furthermore, it is hard to know the present state of affairs, since the coalition headquarters in Afghanistan has stopped publishing the district-level stability assessments that formed the basis for the judgments above. As John Sopko, the Special Inspector General for Afghanistan, complained: "What we are finding is now almost every metric for success or failure is now classified or nonexistent." [14] This follows direction from President Trump, who questioned why reports with operationally useful information would be made public.[15]

Long Wars Are Not a U.S. Strength

The United States has shown that it can engage in long struggles. The Cold War lasted 40 years, and the United States persevered. Similarly, the United States shows no sign of easing up on the struggle against global Islamic terrorism. However, this endurance has not been seen in major armed conflicts. With these, the United States tires after a few years, and the desire to get out may induce it to accept goals much reduced from what it might have otherwise achieved.[16]

It has become commonplace to observe that "the American people give their government and military approximately three years to win or show tangible results. After that, public support for further military effort flags to the point where withdrawal is inevitable."[17] This pessimistic assessment comes from analysis of public opinion polls, which indicate that, absent clear progress towards victory, "as casualties

---

doms-sentinel-i-quarterly-report-to-th/.

12. Bill Roggio and Alexandra Gutowski, "Mapping Taliban Control In Afghanistan," *Long War Journal*, https://www.longwarjournal.org/mapping-taliban-control-in-Afghanistan.

13. Ibid.

14. Katie Bo Williams, "It's getting harder to track U.S. progress in Afghanistan," *Defense One*, April 24, 2019.

15. Rebecca Kheel, "Trump Calls It 'Insane' to Publicly Release Reports Military Watchdog Reports," *Hill*, January 2, 2019, https://thehill.com/policy/defense/423566-trump-its-insane-to-publicly-release-military-watchdog-reports.

16. Mark Cancian, "Winning Hearts and Minds at Home," *Naval Institute Proceedings*, September 2010, https://www.usni.org/magazines/proceedings/2010/september/winning-hearts-and-minds-home.

17. Jim Lacey and Kevin Woods, "Adapt or Die," U.S. Naval Institute, August 1, 2007, https://www.usni.org/magazines/proceedings/2007/august/adapt-or-die; the phrase "three years and out" comes from Steven Metz, "Three Years and You're Out," *National Interest Online*, January 2, 2008.

mount, support decreases"—and that there is little a president can do to reverse this inexorable trend.[18]

The graph below illustrates the basis for such a conclusion. In the three major conflicts of the last 70 years, public support has inevitably eroded as fighting continued without clear progress, despite the vigorous efforts of presidents to sustain that support. (Korea's small uptick in support towards the end occurred when truce talks seemed likely to end the war.)

Figure 5: Public Support for the Wars in Korea, Vietnam, and Iraq

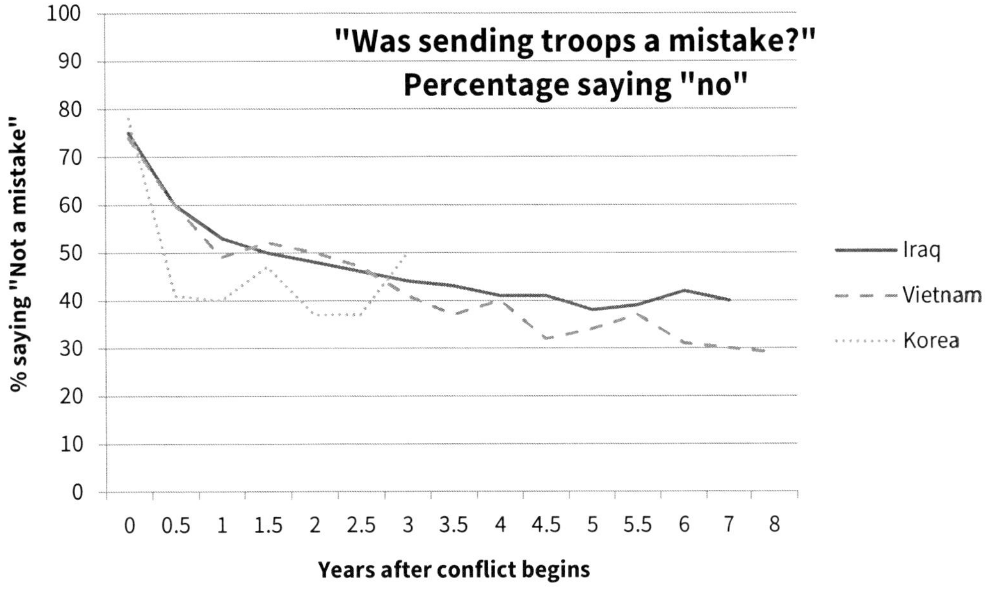

Source: Gallup Organization[19]

Of course, polls are not destiny. Presidents can promote their policies, perhaps easing the erosion of support. Eventually, however, protracted conflict without clear victory discourages the populace, and politics follows public opinion.

Afghanistan was supposed to be different. Because the 9/11 attacks had been planned there, both policymakers and the public viewed intervention as necessary. The harsh and oppressive nature of Taliban governance delegitimized its regime. Our allies were supportive. The United Nations provided strong support through its resolutions, and NATO contributed a military headquarters. Even opponents of the war in Iraq were on board, particularly vocal in contrasting the conflict in Afghanistan ("the good war") with the conflict in Iraq ("the bad war").

18. John Mueller, "The Iraq Syndrome," *Foreign Affairs*, January 29, 2009, https://www.foreignaffairs.com/articles/north-korea/2005-10-01/iraq-syndrome. Mueller has been a persistent researcher on the question of wartime public opinion and political action. See also: John Mueller, *War, Presidents, and Public Opinion* (New York: Wiley, 1973).

19. Polling data from Gallup Organization, retrieved from their web site at www.gallup.com. All were in response to the same question: "Was it a mistake to send U.S. troops to [named conflict]?" (2010 Iraq data from slightly different question.)

Nevertheless, there has been a continuous erosion of public support over time (even among those who saw it as the "good war"), although that erosion has taken longer than the historical three years.

Figure 5: Public Support for the War in Afghanistan

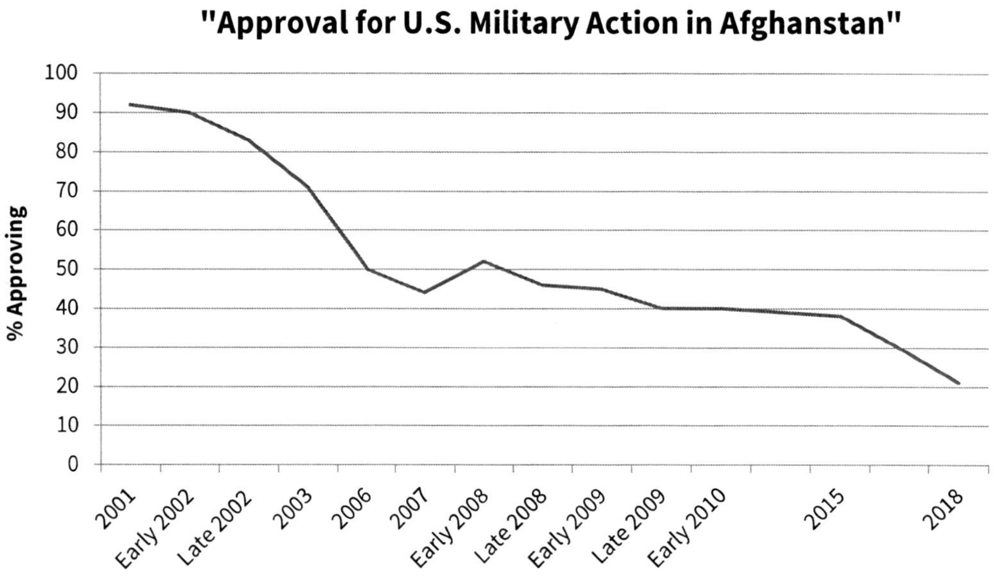

Source: Gallup Organization, CNN/Opinion Research, and Washington Post/ABC News[20]

It's Not All Bad

The record of the coalition intervention in Afghanistan may include many disappointments and a high cost, but its impact has not been entirely negative. Bin Laden is dead, and although Al Qaeda has not been destroyed, it has been badly damaged. Since 2001, there have been no more terrorist attacks from abroad—an important result even if the reasons for the lack of an attack are much broader than just coalition operations in Afghanistan, since this was the primary reason for U.S. intervention there.

For average Afghans, there have been many benefits to quality of life. Considering how poorly Afghanistan was faring on many fronts, the fact that there have been improvements is not a surprise; nevertheless, gains have been dramatic in some areas:

- Afghanistan has held a series of more or less free national elections since 2001[21];

20. Polling data for 2001-2009 from Gallup Organization and CNN/Opinion Research. 2010 data from Washington Post/ABC News. Question was not asked in 2004 or 2005, a reflection of the war's low profile during those years. Note: These polls asked whether respondents "approved or disapproved of US military action in Afghanistan." This question better gets at the public's current opinions than the question, "Was US military action in Afghanistan a mistake?" For Afghanistan, unlike Iraq, the public answers these questions differently. Many people say that the original action in 2001 was not a mistake but that they disapprove of military action today. This is likely because of the memory that the 9/11 attacks originated in Afghanistan. However, what is important today is not an historical judgment about actions in 2001 but what the public will currently support. Question not asked after 2010, instead, data from 2015 and 2018 are for a similar question, "Is the U.S. winning in Afghanistan?" See *Public Opinion on Afghanistan War*, Koch Foundation, October 18, 2018, https://www.charleskochinstitute.org/news/Afghanistan-17-anniversary-poll/.
21. Haidary, Mohammad Shoaib. "By the Numbers: Is Afghanistan's Democracy at Risk?" The Asia Foundation,

- Life expectancy at birth rose from 56 years in 2001 to 64 years in 2017[22];
- Maternal mortality fell from 11 per 1,000 births in 2000, the 4th highest rank in the world, to 3.96 per 1,000 births in 2015, ranked 28th highest[23];
- Infant mortality fell from 88 per 1000 births in 2001 to 51.5 per 1,000 births in 2017, and the under-five mortality rate dropped by almost 46 percent over that time, to 67.9 per 1,000 children[24];
- Sanitation improved, with 39.2 percent of the population having access to at least basic sanitation in 2015, a 15.3 percentage point increase over 2000 levels.[25] Over the same period, the proportion of the population using basic drinking water services rose by 36 percentage points, to 63 percent[26];
- Mobile cellular subscriptions rose from zero in 2001 to almost 24 million in 2017[27];
- GDP rose by 382 percent from 2002 to 2017, to $19.5 billion dollars in current USD equivalent[28];
- Primary school enrollment, as a percentage of target age cohort, has risen from 21.7 percent in 2001 to almost 104 percent in 2017 (more than 100 percent because some overage students are attending).[29] Of students in attendance, the proportion of girls has increased from 0 to 39%[30]; and
- Twenty percent of members of parliament are women.[31]

Were the Benefits Worth the Cost?

This question is unanswerable until Afghanistan reaches some long-term stability. If the gains are permanent, it may be that the costs paid will have been worthwhile. What is clear, however, is that the United States and the Afghan people have paid a high price for the benefits so far.

Furthermore, this may arguably be the wrong question to ask, since it implies that the only road to obtaining these benefits was the full-scale nation-building effort that the coalition embarked on. A better question would be: could there have been less costly ways

December 12, 2018, https://asiafoundation.org/2018/08/15/by-the-numbers-is-afghanistans-democracy-at-risk/.
22. "Life Expectancy at Birth." *The World Bank*, Accessed June 4, 2019. https://databank.worldbank.org/data/source/2/Type/metadata?series=NY.GDP.MKTP.CD&savedlg=1,1&l=en,en,en#. (excludes Tuvalu due to lack of available data)
23. "Trends in Estimates of Maternal Mortality Ratio (maternal Deaths per 100,000 Live Births) 1990-2015," United Nations Children's Fund, February 2017, https://data.unicef.org/topic/maternal-health/maternal-mortality/.
24. "Most Recent Child Mortality Estimates," United Nations Inter-Agency Group for Child Mortality Estimation, accessed June 4, 2019, https://childmortality.org/data.
25. "Water and Sanitation Coverage," UNICEF Drinking Water, Sanitation and Hygiene Database, July 2017, https://data.unicef.org/topic/water-and-sanitation/sanitation/.
26. Ibid.
27. "Mobile Cellular Subscriptions," *World Bank*, Accessed June 4, 2019. https://data.worldbank.org/indicator/IT.CEL.SETS?locations=AF.
28. "GDP (current US$)," The World Bank, accessed June 4, 2019, https://databank.worldbank.org/data/source/2/Type/metadata?series=NY.GDP.MKTP.CD&savedlg=1,1&l=en,en,en#.
29. "School Enrollment, Primary (% Gross)," World Bank, accessed June 4, 2019, https://data.worldbank.org/indicator/SE.PRM.ENRR.
30. "Primary Education, Pupils (% Female)," World Bank, accessed June 19, 2019, https://data.worldbank.org/indicator/SE.PRM.ENRL.FE.ZS.
31. "New Parline: The IPU's Open Data Platform (beta)," New Parline: The IPU's Open Data Platform (beta), Accessed July 01, 2019, https://data.ipu.org/.

to achieve at least some of these benefits? Most of the social and economic improvements were attained through the provision of basic security in Afghanistan and the elimination of Taliban mismanagement. In fact, this alone could also have achieved the key goal of preventing further attacks on the U.S. homeland from groups based in Afghanistan. Thus, a limited goal of political stability and coalition government that included the Taliban might have benefited U.S. and Afghan people nearly as well as the current situation has, without sparking 18 years of war. History cannot be rerun to confirm the truth of this statement. However, this is worth keeping in mind the next time the United States faces a similar problem, as it inevitably will. As this report emphatically seeks to make clear, goals and end states are choices.

3 | End States Drive the Military Effort

U.S. decision-makers faced a key judgment early on. Should they adopt the limited goal of preventing Afghanistan from becoming a launch platform for future attacks on the United States? Or would it be better for the United States to try to reconstruct Afghanistan—i.e., to "nation-build"—so that, by attaining the Western vision of twenty-first-century society and polity, Afghanistan would be structurally less likely to pose a threat to the United States?

Nation-building in Afghanistan, as envisioned by the United States and its international coalition, would entail a wide variety of social and political changes:

- The central government would provide effective governance throughout the entire country;
- The impartial rule of law would operate;
- Political leadership would be chosen through democratic processes;
- Religious differences would be tolerated;
- Speech would be uncensored;
- A market economy would operate;
- Human rights, as the West understood them, would be respected; and
- Women and girls would be empowered.

While these changes were all admirable, nation-building in this context meant imposing the changes by force if necessary, in other words, "nation-building out of the barrel of a gun." This is why General David Petraeus's question—"Tell me how this ends?"—is fundamental.[32] Knowing where you want to go determines how long the road will take, and how difficult it will be to get there. Unfortunately, for the conflict in Afghanistan, the military implications of different end states were never fully articulated, or even considered.

32. Rick Atkinson, "The Long, Blinding Road to War," *Washington Post*, March 7, 2004.

Limited Initial Objectives

The United States began with limited goals, as demonstrated by numerous excerpts from former secretary of defense Donald Rumsfeld's memoirs:

> "Our primary goal was to prevent additional attacks against America and our interests."[33]
>
> "It's my point of view that we need to limit our mission to getting the terrorists who find their way to Afghanistan. We ought not to make a career out of transforming Afghanistan."[34]
>
> "Local Afghans and Iraqis know far better than we do how to form and at what pace to evolve their societies. Solving corruption in Afghanistan or building a secular democracy in the Middle East are not America's problems to tackle. They are not our broken societies to fix."[35]
>
> "My position was that we were not in Afghanistan to transform a deeply conservative Islamic culture into a model of liberal modality. We were not there to eradicate corruption or to end poppy cultivation. We were not there to take ownership of Afghanistan's problems, tempting though it was for many Americans of goodwill. Instead, Afghans would need to take charge of their own fate. Afghans would build their society the way they wanted. With our coalition allies, we would assist them within reason where we were able."[36]

Indeed, as a candidate George W. Bush had foresworn nation-building, criticizing the Clinton administration's efforts during the 1990s: We need to do is convince people who live [there] to build [their own] nations. Our military is meant to fight and win wars. And when it gets overextended, morale drops. I strongly believe we need to keep a presence in NATO, but I'm going to be judicious as to how to use the military. It needs to be in our vital interests, the mission needs to be clear, and the exit strategy obvious.[37]

President Bush reiterated that sentiment later, when operations to overthrow the Taliban were concluding: "I oppose using the military for nation-building. Once the job is done, our forces are not peacekeepers. We ought to put in place a U.N. protection [organization] and leave."[38]

On the military side, General Richard Myers, then-chairman of the Joint Chiefs of Staff, made the same point in his 2002 posture statement: "Our objectives in this war are simple: to disrupt and destroy global terrorist organizations, eliminate safe havens for terrorists, and prevent access to WMD by terrorist groups."[39]

---

33. Donald Rumsfeld, *Known and Unknown: A Memoir* (New York: Knopf, 2014), 352.
34. Ibid., 398.
35. Ibid., 682
36. Ibid., 724.
37. *Presidential Candidates' Debate*, C-SPAN, October 11, 2000, https://www.c-span.org/video/?c4315725/george-w-bush-nation-building. Quotation shortened for clarity.
38. Bob Woodward, *Bush at War* (New York: Simon and Schuster, 2002), 237.
39. U.S. Congress, Senate, Committee on Armed Services, *Department of Defense Authorization for Appropriations for Fiscal Year 2003 by Richard Myers*, 107th Cong., 2nd sess., 2002, https://www.govinfo.gov/content/pkg/CHRG-107shrg81922/html/CHRG-107shrg81922.htm.

There was a coherent initial strategy. The Taliban regime would be overthrown rapidly, the footprint would be light, the troop levels would be low, and the United States would leave quickly. Lieutenant General Michael DeLong, deputy commander of Central Command during the early period, described this in his memoirs: "We had designed our war plan for Afghanistan with a small number of troops; keeping our presence down was key to keeping the peoples' goodwill . . . [Shelton and Rumsfeld] wanted a campaign that inflicted minimal damage so that the country could be quickly reconstructed and put in the hands of a strong, stable Afghan government."[40]

However, there was no discussion about where that new Afghan government would come from or who would create it. Gen. Myers noted the failing in his memoirs: "The White House had made it clear that America would not engage in 'nation-building' in Afghanistan. Our mission was to topple the Taliban regime and destroy Al Qaeda, not nurture civilian institutions. Having been through these discussions before, I was not at all sure we could topple the Taliban and eradicate Al Qaeda and then simply leave. I hoped that other nations, international organizations, and nongovernmental organizations would take up the post-conflict effort."[41] Unfortunately, that did not happen.

The 2002–2004 Shift

Despite Rumsfeld's desire to keep the mission limited in scope, and Bush's apparent predisposition to do so as well, the mission expanded to embrace a broad nation-building agenda. This was not in response to Taliban resurgence, which would not occur until 2004–2006. Rather, it arose from a variety of other causes. Foremost among these was a disappointment in the weakness of the Afghan government, which was ineffective and whose reach into the countryside was limited; "failed states" such as these were viewed as security threats to the United States. There was also a recognition of how damaged the Afghan economy was after years of civil war.

Furthermore, there was a desire among decision-makers to create a modern society in Afghanistan. At that moment in its history, 2002–2003, everything seemed possible: the Taliban had been vanquished, and the Western coalition and Afghan elites could reshape Afghan society and politics without the need to accommodate other views.

Finally, a fair amount of hubris went into this decision, as will be detailed later. Lessons that could have been learned from the Soviet experience in Afghanistan were ignored, as was the history of occupations and the Taliban. As the ancient Greeks warned, hubris begets nemesis.

President Bush himself signaled that expansion early, saying in 2002: "We know that true peace will only be achieved when we give the Afghan people the means to achieve their own aspirations. Peace will be achieved by helping Afghanistan develop its own stable government. Peace will be achieved by helping Afghanistan train and develop its own national army. And peace will be achieved through an education system for boys and girls, which works. We're working hard in Afghanistan. We're clearing minefields. We're

---

40. Lieutenant General Michael DeLong, *Inside CENTCOM: The Unvarnished Truth about the Wars in Afghanistan and Iraq* (Washington DC: Regnery Publishing, 2004), 23, 59.
41. Myers, *Posture Statement*, 174.

rebuilding roads. We're improving medical care. And we will work to help Afghanistan develop an economy that can feed its people without feeding the world's demand for drugs."[42] The shift was captured in a 2004 document entitled "Accelerating Success in Afghanistan," which laid out a nation-building program.[43] Gen. Myers also noted the shift in his memoirs: "Although the administration had initially sought to leave the 'nation-building' challenge of Operation Enduring Freedom to others, it had become clear that we would be needed for the indefinite future."[44]

Public statements by senior military officers came to reflect this expanded set of goals. However, there was no recognition in these statements that there had been any change to the mission's initial limited goals:

Table 3: Statements by Senior Military Officers on Goals in Afghanistan

Date	Quote	Who
2/7/2006	"[Our goals in Afghanistan are to] assist Afghans at the local level in building a stable and free society . . . Develop the security capabilities of the fledgling democracies in advance regional stability."[45]	Gen. Peter Pace, Chairman of the Joint Chiefs of Staff
10/4/2006	"Anything we do militarily is perishable if it's not accompanied by reconstruction. Where we are able to put in good governance, good leaders, and good governors, the Taliban drifts off into [other] areas."[46]	Gen. James Jones, Supreme Allied Commander, Europe
3/3/2015	"Afghanistan is headed in the right direction towards a fully functioning inclusive government . . ."[47]	Gen. Martin Dempsey, Chairman of the Joint Chiefs of Staff

Crucially, *there is no evidence that military and civilian leaders ever discussed what this policy change implied for the duration and intensity of the conflict.*[48] Former secretary of state Condoleezza Rice, for example, devotes only one paragraph to the shift in her 730-page memoir.[49] Former vice president Dick Cheney never mentions the shift in his memoir at all.[50] As Lieutenant General Daniel Bolger noted in his dissection of the wars, "[Senior military officers] assumed the Bush administration understood that this would be an effort of decades.

42. George W. Bush, "President Outlines War Effort: Speech at Virginia Military Institute," National Archives and Records Administration, April 17, 2002.
43. For an unclassified overview, see NSC memo "Accelerating Success in Afghanistan in 2004 - an Assessment," January 18, 2005, http://papers.rumsfeld.com/endnotes/chapter-47/
44. Richard B. Myers, *Eyes on the Horizon: Serving on the Front Lines of National Security* (New York: Simon and Schuster, 2009), 221.
45. General Peter Pace, "Posture Statement of General Peter Pace, USMC Chairman of the Joint Chiefs of Staff," speech to the Senate Armed Services Committee of the 109th Congress, February 7, 2006, https://www.globalsecurity.org/military/library/congress/2006_hr/060207-pace.pdf.
46. General James. L. Jones, "NATO's Role in Afghanistan," speech to the Council on Foreign Relations, Washington DC, October 4, 2006.
47. General Martin Dempsey, "Posture Statement of General Martin E. Dempsey, USA, 18th Chairman of the Joint Chiefs of Staff," speech to the Senate Armed Services Committee of the 114th Congress, March 3, 2015, https://www.armed-services.senate.gov/imo/media/doc/Dempsey_03-03-15.pdf.
48. One former senior official interviewed for this project stated that a principals meeting of the NSC had been scheduled on this topic, but that it was canceled because of DoD opposition.
49. Condoleezza Rice, *No Higher Honor: A Memoir of My Years in Washington* (New York: Crown Publishers, 2011).
50. Dick Cheney, *In My Time: A Personal and Political Memoir* (New York: Simon and Schuster, 2011).

They assumed wrongly. Successor commanders in both theaters [Iraq and Afghanistan]—Petraeus, Odierno, McChrystal, Allen, Dunford—made equally poor assumptions that, despite every indication to the contrary, the Obama administration would commit to major long-term U.S. troop deployments. Somehow, on this most vital issue of all, during hundreds of hours of meetings, the uniforms and the suits managed to talk past each other."[51]

This occurred notwithstanding the many statements by general officers that the war would be long and General Dempsey's later observation that "when objectives change, we should simply recognize this and adapt accordingly. Sometimes changing objectives is portrayed as mission failure, when, in fact, in a protracted campaign, the likelihood of renegotiating objectives is 100 percent."[52]

The expansion of the mission was reinforced by the Afghan constitution, established in 2002, which embodied nation-building principles, wrapped in a cover of traditional Islam ("Believing firmly in Almighty God, relying on His divine will and adhering to the Holy religion of Islam"—Preamble).[53] Its provisions were important because they provided the formal goal for the U.S. and coalition military effort—i.e., this is what we were fighting for. Some examples of nation-building principles incorporated into the document include:

- "Observing the United Nations charter as well as the Universal Declaration of Human Rights." (Preamble)
- "Followers of other faiths shall be free within the bounds of law in the exercise and performance of their religious rituals." (Article 2)
- "The state shall design and implement effective programs for developing industries . . ." (Article 13)
- "The state, within its financial means, shall design and implement effective programs to develop agriculture . . . And [make] provision of housing . . ." (Article 14)
- "The state shall adopt necessary measures to foster education at all levels." (Article 17)
- "The citizens of Afghanistan, man and woman, have equal rights and duties before the law." (Article 22)
- "The state shall respect and protect liberty as well as human dignity." (Article 24)
- "Freedom of expression shall be inviolable." (Article 34)
- "Education is the right of all citizens of Afghanistan, which shall be offered up to the BA level in state educational institutes free of charge by the state." (Article 43)
- "The state shall devise and implement effective programs to create and foster balanced education for women . . ." (Article 44)
- "The state shall provide free preventative healthcare and treatment of diseases as well as medical facilities to all citizens in accordance with the provisions of the law." (Article 52)

51. Bolger, *Why We Lost*, 430.
52. R.D. Hooker, Jr and Joseph J. Collins, "From the Chairman: an Interview with Martin Dempsey," *Joint Force Quarterly* 78 (July 2015).
53. "The Constitution of Afghanistan," ratified January 26, 2004, http://www.afghanembassy.com.pl/afg/images/pliki/TheConstitution.pdf.

- "The government, in preserving the principles of centralism, shall transfer necessary powers, in accordance with the law, to local administrations . . ." (Article 137)

Proponents note that the constitution was not forced on Afghanistan but arose from its own representatives. However, it is also true that the constitution strongly reflected the views of educated and westernized Afghans who, as will be discussed later, did not represent the views of the countryside, where the majority of the population lived. Indeed, the "Rome group," a major player in the drafting, was made up of Afghan leaders who had fled to Europe and the United States. What the drafters of the constitution likely had in mind was re-creating a version of Afghanistan's brief "golden age," which was a period between 1964 (when King Zahir Shah promulgated a liberal constitution) and 1973 (when a coup overthrew Zahir, the constitution was abolished, and the country descended into instability).[54]

All of these nation-building principles make sense, and they reflect the way that modern democracies believe societies should be ordered. Deleting any of these provisions from the constitution would have seemed an affront to Western notions of decency, subject to harsh criticism by the coalition governments. After all, what were the coalition troops fighting for if not for these kinds of values? These nation-building goals were particularly salient to the NATO allies, whose forces became increasingly important after 2006, since their human-rights-conscious electorates needed a strong justification for their involvement in the war.

The United States and the coalition believed that these provisions were modest, and they eagerly supported them. Although some provisions were known to spark debate in particular Western societies (government-provided education and health care, for example), none were expected to inspire a violent reaction. Thus, the constitution seemed sensible, and its provisions were viewed as relatively uncontroversial.

In fact, the constitution—and the coalition's associated nation-building effort—entailed profound changes to Afghan political and social life. It proposed to take a society that was politically decentralized, religiously devout, socially conservative, clan and tribe based, and patriarchal, and to turn it into the Western vision of a twenty-first--century society. Far from constituting modest social and political changes, this vision would change an Afghan's relationship with his family, his government, and his God.

In the nineteenth century, Western colonial interventions brought with them the imposition of modernity, the creation of unified states, and the spread of Christianity. At the time, these actions were considered reasonable; even in retrospect, they look inevitable. Today, interventions impose digital technologies, representative government, and human rights. Many among the Western elites would be horrified to think that their efforts to bring contemporary values to developing countries might be seen as an analog to the nineteenth-century work of colonialists—but to peoples on the receiving end, they can look quite similar.

54. Barnett R. Rubin, "Afghanistan's Constitutional Process 2001-2004," Kennedy School of Government, Harvard University, https://sites.hks.harvard.edu/fs/pnorris/Classes/Rubin%20paper.pdf.

When "No Nation-Building" Is Nation-Building

The Obama administration had originally stated that it would not pursue "nation-building" but instead focus on eliminating Al Qaeda. In a March 2009 speech on Afghanistan, President Obama laid out his goal: "I want the American people to understand that we have a clear and focused goal: to disrupt, dismantle and defeat al Qaeda in Pakistan and Afghanistan, and to prevent their return to either country in the future."[55] This narrow focus followed a recommendation from Secretary Gates: "In my January 26 [2009] meeting with Obama, I told him that we should have 'no grandiose aspirations' in Afghanistan because we just wanted to prevent the country from again becoming a source of threats to U.S. or our allies."[56]

The problem is that the administration could not bring itself to give up the broader effort, to remake Afghanistan. In this same 2009 speech, President Obama laid out a variety of goals—the "comprehensive strategy,"—that, in sum, did in fact constitute nation-building:

- "For the Afghan people, a return to Taliban rule would condemn their country to brutal governance, international isolation, a paralyzed economy, and the denial of basic human rights to the Afghan people—especially women and girls."
- "Our efforts will fail in Afghanistan and Pakistan if we don't invest in their future."
- "[T]o advance security, opportunity, and justice—not just in Kabul, but from the bottom up in the provinces—we need agricultural specialists and educators, engineers and lawyers. That's how we can help the Afghan government serve its people and develop an economy that isn't dominated by illicit drugs."
- "[We will] create opportunity zones in the border regions to develop the economy and bring hope to places plagued with violence."
- "We will seek a new compact with the Afghan government that cracks down on corrupt behavior . . . "
- "We will continue to support the basic human rights of all Afghans—including women and girls."[57]

Further, the Afghan constitution, referred to by President Obama in his speech, embodied extensive nation-building principles, as described earlier.

General Stanley A. McChrystal's strategic plan for Afghanistan accepted these end state goals without comment: "ISAF's strategy is consistent with . . . President Obama's strategy to disrupt, dismantle, and eventually defeat Al Qaeda and prevent their return to Afghanistan."[58]

However, McChrystal's strategy showed the same bifurcation that Obama's did. On the one hand, it framed the struggle as a limited conflict against Al Qaeda. On the other hand, it

---

55. Office of the Press Secretary, "Remarks by the President on a New Strategy for Afghanistan and Pakistan," The White House, March 27, 2009, https://obamawhitehouse.archives.gov/the-press-office/remarks-president-a-new-strategy-Afghanistan-and-pakistan.
56. Gates, *Duty: Memoirs of a Secretary at War* (Knopf, 2014), 337.
57. All quotes from Office of the Press Secretary, "Remarks by the President on a New Strategy for Afghanistan and Pakistan," op. cit.
58. "COMISAF Initial Assessment (Unclassified)," *The Washington Post*, September 21, 2009, http://www.washingtonpost.com/wp-dyn/content/article/2009/09/21/AR2009092100110.html.

embraced broad transformational goals: "access to justice," "expansion of accountable and transparent governance," "creating sustainable jobs, agricultural opportunity, and market access," "facilitating governance and elections," and "countering the nexus of narcotics, corruption, insurgency and criminality." [59]

As noted earlier, these transformational goals make sense. They reflect the way Western societies believe that society and politics should be organized. Eliminating any of these goals would constitute a moral affront. The problem is not the goals themselves, but the prolonged and intense effort required to implement them in traditional societies.

McChrystal's formulation points to a fundamental confusion in strategy: who was the enemy? Was it Al Qaeda, which had attacked the United States and which continued to threaten the West with calls for jihad? Their numbers in Afghanistan were small, but they were irreconcilable. That implied a narrow set of goals for the campaign. Or was the enemy the Taliban, whose oppressive rule and economic mismanagement had made conditions so bad for the average Afghan? Although the Taliban had sheltered Al Qaeda, they themselves never attacked or even threated the United States.[60]

A serious but unintended effect of ignoring the dichotomy between stated and actual goals was severe tension between the Obama White House—which wanted a time- and troop-limited commitment—and the military leadership—which argued for more troops and more time to implement the expansive White House goals. On the one hand, the White House saw the military as trying to "box it in" by limiting options to those that required large troop increases. On the other hand, the military thought the White House was trying to achieve victory on the cheap. Because of this, while the 2009 review of Afghanistan policy did give rise to a vigorous debate, the discussion focused almost entirely on the number of troops rather than goals and end state.[61]

During this 2009 review, Vice-President Joseph Biden raised the possibility of a change in strategy, arguing for a limited "counterterrorism" strategy that focused on Al Qaeda. Meanwhile, others, particularly civilian and military officials in the Department of Defense, argued for a broad "counterinsurgency" strategy focused on the Taliban. Despite many hours of meetings and an intense review process, neither Biden nor the Department of Defense appears to have fully made the connection to end states. Biden, for example, was focused on the political sustainability of the war; he did not acknowledge that a focus on counterterrorism would entail easing some of the administration's cherished nation-building goals. Rather, he wanted to have both nation-building and a large reduction of force commitments.[62]

Another dissenting voice, Ambassador Karl Eikenberry (a retired Army lieutenant general and former commander in Afghanistan), opposed the surge in troops because "the proposed troop increases will bring vastly increased costs and an indefinite large-scale U.S. military role . . . increase Afghan dependency and run counter to our strategic purposes

59. All quotation from COMISAF, ibid.
60. Bolger makes this point extensively in *Why We Lost*.
61. See, for example, Stanley McChrystal, *My Share of the Task: A Memoir* (Penguin Books, 2013), especially chapter 19 "Decide".
62. Bob Woodward, *Obama's Wars* (New York: Simon and Schuster, 2010), 160-161. See also: Gates, *Memoirs*, op. cit., 385.

of Afghanizing and civilianizing government functions [there]."[63] However, although Eikenberry noted the weakness of the Afghan government, he did not propose or even hint at any limitation to the end state.

A Classic Case of Mission Creep

The expansion of goals in Afghanistan constitutes a classic example of "mission creep," that is, an operation that began with a limited set of goals, which incrementally expanded once on the ground. The military's acquiescence to mission creep in Afghanistan occurred despite extensive literature warning against it, much of which had arisen in the 1990s after the tragic experience in Somalia. In 1992, the United States had intervened in Somalia to ease a humanitarian crisis and avoid mass starvation; however, the mission later expanded to include suppressing warlords and trying to bring stability and effective governance to that failed state. This effort culminated in an ill-fated 1993 operation to capture one of the warlords, Mohamed Farrah Adeed, during which 18 U.S. citizens were killed, 73 wounded, and several helicopters shot down, in the now infamous "Black Hawk down" event.[64]

Looking back on this experience, Ambassador Robert B. Oakley summed up what many others—indeed, an entire literature—had observed: "'Mission creep' is the unconscious or deliberate assumption of policy goals or operational objectives that commit resources beyond what our interests call for . . . A way to guard against it is to be sure that our policy goals stay as limited as our interests and that operational objectives coincide with policy goals at every stage of involvement."[65] The problem is not that missions creep, but that they creep stealthily, without a policy debate to ensure that goals and interests are aligned.

General Colin Powell had similarly warned about this in the 1990s. His "Powell doctrine," articulated to shape future interventions after his experience of the Vietnam war and the disastrous 1983 intervention in Lebanon, included two relevant items: "do we have a clear attainable objective" and "is there a plausible exit strategy to avoid endless entanglement." He pointedly stated: "We must not, for example, send military forces into a crisis with an unclear mission they cannot accomplish, such as we did when we sent the U.S. Marines into Lebanon in 1983."[66] The 1984 "Weinberger doctrine" had similar cautions, upon, which Powell had built.[67]

A Shift to Help Peace Negotiations?

A shift back to something like the limited goals of the early Rumsfeld era may be taking place today. Although the Trump administration has not formally changed U.S. goals in Afghanistan, it is pushing negotiations harder, despite the fact that any public statement implying that it is giving up on nation-building goals would be met with strong

63. Ambassador Karl Eikenberry, *Coin Strategy: Civilian Concerns*, U.S. Department of State cable, November 6, 2009.
64. Mark Bowden, *Black Hawk Down: a Story of Modern War* (New York: Grove Press, 1999).
65. Ambassador Robert B. Oakley, *Two Perspectives on Interventions and Humanitarian Operations* (Strategic Studies Institute, Army War College, 1997), https://ssi.armywarcollege.edu/pdffiles/00309.pdf.
66. All quotations from Colin Powell, "U.S. Forces: The Challenges Ahead," *Foreign Affairs* 71, no. 5 (Winter 1992): 32–45.
67. Caspar Weinberger, "The Uses of Military Power," speech delivered at the National Press Club, November 28, 1984.

opposition. The maximalist nation-building goals espoused by the United States, its coalition, and the Afghan government will not be achievable, given the relative weakness of their negotiating position. Some observers believe that the administration will reduce its expectations, aiming instead for a simple agreement providing for U.S. and allied withdrawal, some sort of coalition government, and a Taliban commitment to prevent future terrorist attacks originating from Afghanistan.[68]

President Trump has certainly added to this speculation, repeatedly expressing his desire to withdraw U.S. forces. Before attaining the presidency, he sent out a dozen tweets with similar themes, such as: "We have wasted an enormous amount of blood and treasure in Afghanistan. Their government has zero appreciation. Let's get out!"[69]

Trump's frustration has continued to the present time, despite his authorizing additional forces: "I inherited a total mess in Syria and Afghanistan, the 'Endless Wars' of unlimited spending and death. During my campaign, I said, very strongly, that these wars must finally end. We spend $50 Billion a year in Afghanistan and have hit them so hard that we are now talking peace. . ."[70]

Yet, despite the limitation of goals currently being implied, it is unclear whether military advice about duration and intensity has changed. As will be discussed later, military leaders have continued to ask for additional forces and more time. Further, NATO statements contain the same wording about nation-building as before.

On the other hand, some experts have perceived a shift of military operations away from counterinsurgency, instead moving towards punishing the Taliban to make them more receptive to a negotiated settlement.[71] NATO press releases hint at such a shift: "Afghan National Defense and Security Forces . . . and the international community continue to apply judicious military pressure to enable the Taliban's eventual reconciliation, reintegration, and realignment."[72]

If military advice has, indeed, changed with the change in goals, that would be evidence of flexibility in strategic thinking. Time will tell.

Using Military Forces for Nation-Building

Despite criticism that values cannot be forced on people, history shows that values can, in fact, be established at the point of a bayonet. The United States did that in Germany, Japan, and South Korea: none of these countries had democratic regimes or a commitment to human rights before U.S. occupation. Now all are stable and wealthy nations with strong democratic institutions and protections of individual rights. It is a tribute to the Germans, Japanese, and South Koreans that they were able to do this with the help of the United

68. Jonathan Schroden, "Weighing the Costs of War and Peace in Afghanistan," War on the Rocks, March 21, 2019.
69. @realdonaldtrump, 12:06 PM November 21, 2013.
70. @realdonaldtrump, 5:23 AM February 1, 2019.
71. For an example, see: Jonathan Schroden, "Military Pressure and the Body Counts in Afghanistan," War on the Rocks, May 17, 2019.
72. NATO Operation Resolute Support Press Release, *U.S. Forces – Afghanistan October 2018 Strike Summary*, November 4, 2018, https://rs.nato.int/news-center/press-releases/2018-press-releases/us-forces-afghanistan-october-2018-strike-summary.aspx.

States and its military. However, all these efforts entailed long-term commitments, and U.S. troops are still in these countries 70 years after the military events that initiated them.

On the other hand, even with a major effort, success is not guaranteed. The counterexample is Vietnam, where the United States made all of the same efforts it made in Germany, Japan, and South Korea: developing the economy, fostering democratic elections, encouraging human rights, reforming agriculture, and building the rule of law. The effort failed in Vietnam. Wearied by the long, indecisive conflict, the United States gave up after 15 years, opting to withdraw its troops in 1973 and ending aid in 1974. Perhaps rebuilding societies and cultures during wartime is just too difficult;the United States had the benefit of peace when rebuilding Germany, Japan, and South Korea.

Haiti is another cautionary tale. U.S. involvement has been sustained, with long occupations, extensive development assistance, and continuous encouragement of democratic institutions. Despite all this, Haiti remains poor, badly governed, and authoritarian.

The literature about nation-building is too extensive to do justice to it here. The bottom line is this: success is sometimes possible, but there are no guarantees, even with great efforts.

Political and Cultural Transformation Is a Multi-Generational Effort

Transforming politics, society, and culture takes a long time. The transformation of Afghanistan envisioned by those who advocate for nation-building will take decades, perhaps even generations of U.S. military presence. In the present report, two generations (50 years) is being used as the notional duration for nation-building. The reason for two generations is that old attitudes and loyalties will still surround the first generation, preventing it from fully embracing change; it is the second generation, growing up surrounded by the new attitudes and loyalties and therefore accepting them as normal, that will fully reflect social transformation.

Two examples are relevant here. The first is South Korea. Like Afghanistan, it was poor and devastated by a civil war, with little industry and a highly traditional culture. South Korea began its transformation into a modern state under U.S. tutelage in 1945, when the post-World War II occupation began. That transformation accelerated after the Korean war, and South Korea's economic maturity might be marked by its admittance to the Organization for Economic Cooperation and Development (OECD) in 1996. Its political maturity might be marked by the first peaceful transition of power between parties as a result of election results, which occurred in 1998 when the long-dominant Grand National Party/Democratic Liberal Party ceded power to the National Congress for New Politics. As for South Korea's socio-cultural maturity, that might be marked by the 2005 revision to the constitution, which abolished the Confucian senior male family-head system. So, if we take South Korea as a model for Afghanistan, we can estimate that the transformation will take 50 to 60 years.

The second example is Afghanistan itself. Despite $20 billion in development aid and the intense efforts of a wide range of governmental and nongovernmental organizations over 18 years, Afghanistan remains corrupt, tribal, and socially conservative. Clearly, full transformation will take a lot longer.[73] Transforming an Islamic society is particularly challenging. While Islam provides its adherents with a strong guide for social and community conduct, Islamic majority nations have struggled to build modern societies.

The long timeline of transformations, along with the particular challenges of modernization in Afghanistan, raise the question of what constitutes an "Afghan good enough." How much transformation would be enough? If Afghanistan could look like Egypt—a fairly modern economy but still relatively poor, Islamic but tolerating other religions, sophisticated in urban centers but traditional in the countryside, with elections and some representation but still highly authoritarian—would that be good enough?

The Void in Military Doctrine

FM 3-24 INSURGENCIES AND COUNTERING INSURGENCIES AND OTHER JOINT PUBLICATIONS

One reason for the military's blindness to the importance of end states is that the celebrated counterinsurgency doctrine manual (*Insurgencies and Countering Insurgencies*, FM 3-24) does not discuss it, nor does the slightly updated 2016 version that is currently in effect.[74] The manual, originally written in 2006 by a team under Gen. Petraeus, was intended to respond to the intensifying insurgency in Iraq. Gen. Petraeus used it as his tactical and operational guide when he returned to Iraq in 2006. When violence declined substantially after this troop surge as a result of the new tactics, the manual gained celebrity status. Indeed, it is one of the few military field manuals available for sale to the public through Amazon.

Because of its original design as an operational and tactical guide for Iraq, the manual focuses on elements relevant to that conflict (despite a name change for the 2016 version from *Counterinsurgency* to *Insurgencies and Countering Insurgencies*, with the view of broadening its application). It therefore has chapters on command-and-control, planning, intelligence, operational approaches to counterinsurgency, working with host nations, assessments, and legal considerations.

The manual mentions achieving "strategic objectives," but never says what they are or how they are chosen. [75] It notes that an "end" for the campaign is to "support strategic goals and end state defined by policymakers," but does not discuss what those end states might be.[76] It does note that U.S. involvement could take place on a sliding scale, including indirect approaches that emphasize building capacity in the host nation. However, it never describes how the choice of strategic goals and objectives might affect the military conduct of the campaign.

The default strategic goal in the manual implies a broad nation-building effort:

> Defeating an insurgency requires a blend of both civilian and military efforts that address both assisting the host nation government in defeating the insurgents on

---

73. "$20 billion in aid" from SIGAR, Quarterly Report to Congress, Reconstruction Update, op cit.
74. U.S. Department of the Army, Headquarters, FM 3-24/MCWP 3-02 *Insurgencies and Countering Insurgencies*, Department of the Army, 2016, https://www.marines.mil/Portals/59/Publications/MCWP%203-02%20Formerly%20MCWP%203-33.5.pdf?ver=2017-09-26-114147-930.
75. Ibid., 1-2.
76. Ibid.

> the battlefield and enabling the host nation in addressing the root causes of the insurgency. Moreover, after large scale combat or in the ungoverned space, there may not be a functioning host nation government. In those cases, U.S. forces must work with population groups in the area and enable them to build government capacity.

In part, this void in FM 3-24 is understandable, given that it is a "field manual" and not a national planning document. However, the omission means that there is no standing for a discussion about how military planning might be affected by implementing particular goals— eliminating corruption, strengthening the central government, encouraging religious pluralism, or ensuring human rights, for example.

Other doctrinal manuals, like JP 1 *Doctrine of the Armed Forces of the United States*, JP 3-0 *Joint Operations*, and JP 5-0 *Joint Planning*, do nothing to fill this void. Indeed, the lack of any discussion regarding how choices about end states and goals might drive a campaign is striking. The text below is typical: while it notes that there is such a thing as an end state, it does not discuss how different choices affect the construct of a campaign, nor does it illustrate what those choices might be. Instead, the documents state that the president makes the choice and the military commanders implement it.

> Based on the President's strategic objectives, the supported CCDR [combatant commander] develops and proposes termination criteria—the specified conditions approved by the President or SecDef that must be met before a named operation or campaign can be concluded. These termination criteria help define the desired military end state, which normally represents a point in time or a set of conditions beyond which the president does not require the military instrument of national power as the primary means to achieve remaining national objectives.[77]

Is There Any Real Choice About End States?

Some of the literature implies that nation-building is inevitable. Jeffrey Record, professor at the Air War College, made this argument: "The United States is free to choose most of its overseas military interventions, but it is not free to select their duration and outcome . . . Military intervention imposes post-hostilities political responsibilities."[78] This sentiment has appeared colloquially as "the Pottery Barn rule: you break it, you own it."[79]

The Commission on Post-Conflict Reconstruction expressed a similar perspective:

> As much as some in the United States would like to avoid involvement in nation building, failed states are a reality that cannot be wished away. Indeed, some of the possible candidates for failure in coming years are countries in which the United States already has a defined national security interest—from Iraq and the Occupied Territories in the Middle East to North Korea and Cuba. As the situation

77. Joint Chiefs of Staff, JP 3-0 *Joint Operations* (2017), I-7, 8, https://www.jcs.mil/Portals/36/Documents/Doctrine/pubs/jp3_0ch1.pdf?ver=2018-11-27-160457-910.
78. Jeffrey Record, "Exit Strategy Delusions," Parameters (Winter 2001–2002): 21–27.
79. Colin Powell referred to this rule, apparently apocryphal, as an explanation for why the United States needed to rebuild societies after overthrowing the government. See, Safire, William. "If You Break It..." *New York Times*, October 17, 2004. https://www.nytimes.com/2004/10/17/magazine/if-you-break-it.html.

in Afghanistan has demonstrated, the United States and the international community ignore collapsed or weak states at their peril.[80]

Full consideration of this topic goes far beyond this study, but a short discussion is needed to make the point that viable choices about end states are available to decision-makers. Nation-building, and the long stabilization/counterinsurgency campaigns that go with it, are not inevitable.

The argument against rapid withdrawal is that it risks state collapse. A "failed state" then threatens the security of the United States by becoming a haven for terrorists and criminals. A recent example is Libya: coalition forces departed after overthrowing the Qaddafi regime, and the result has been years of chaos and civil war. For some observers, the implication of this and of similar experiences—Bosnia, Kosovo, Haiti, and many sub-Saharan African countries—is that only a full-scale and long-term occupation, and the nation-building that goes with it, can guarantee success after a regime change.

However, there are examples to the contrary. For example, immediate withdrawal can be successful if there is a legitimate government ready to step in. This was the situation in 1991 after the U.S.-led coalition drove Saddam Hussein's forces out of Kuwait. The Kuwaiti government was able to move in smoothly and rapidly, restore order and governance, and allow the coalition to leave.

There are also intermediate options between nation-building and withdrawal. The British Raj provides an example. The Raj refers to the British rule in India, which lasted approximately 200 years from the mid-eighteenth century to Indian independence in 1948. The British ruled lightly, with only 34,000 troops and occupying a nation of 300 million.[81] It was able to do this because it did not seek to overthrow the local power structure or to replace the existing culture. Princes were allowed to rule their domains as subordinate "princely states," and customs were allowed to continue unchanged with two exceptions: the British suppressed suttee, the custom of a widow throwing herself onto her husband's funeral pyre, and the thugee, a religious sect that murdered innocent bystanders as part of its religious ritual. The British did not impose Christianity—the nineteenth-century version of universal human rights—on the country, although it did allow missionaries to operate on their own, nor did it attack the caste system, which was abhorrent to Europeans but deeply embedded in the local culture.[82]

This paper does not aim to settle the difficult and contentious issue of end states, occupations, and associated military efforts. The point, however, is that all of these things are choices.

---

80. Commission on Post-Conflict Reconstruction, *Play to Win: Final Report of the Bipartisan Commission on Post-Conflict Reconstruction* (Washington, DC/Arlington, VA: Center for Strategic and International Studies and the Association of the U.S. Army, 2003), https://csis-prod.s3.amazonaws.com/s3fs-public/legacy_files/files/media/csis/pubs/playtowin.pdf.
81. James Morris, *Pax Britannica: An Imperial Progress* (London: Folio Society, 1992); James Morris, *Pax Britannica: Climax of an Empire* (London: Folio Society, 1992).
82. For a detailed discussion of the Raj, see James Morris, *Pax Britannica: An Imperial Progress* (London: Folio Society, 1992) and James Morris, *Pax Britannica: Climax of an Empire* (London: Folio Society, 1992).

4 | The Effect of Nation-Building on Military Advice

When senior military officers were faced with the expanded mission of nation-building in Afghanistan, they found themselves in a difficult position. They warned that the conflict would be lengthy, but they did not foresee two decades of commitment. And although the situation on the ground was deteriorating, they expressed confidence in the campaign's progress, a public stance parodied by military humorists. The tension between civil and military expectations did spark important discussions, but these focused on the number of troops that should be deployed; the relationship between desired end state and necessary military effort was not addressed, and there is no sign that military leadership ever tried to address it.

The caveat for this section is that it is written from histories, memoirs, and public documents. It does not and cannot derive information from private advice given by senior military leaders if it was not described in their subsequent writing. As Gen. Myers, former chairman of the Joint Chiefs of Staff, says in his memoirs: "Most military advice to the senior civilian leadership is never revealed publicly."[83] What gives the CSIS team confidence in its assessment is that it has reviewed the literature broadly. Whatever private opinions the senior military leadership may have held—and many were personally critical of the direction of the conflicts—any major policy discussion on this subject that occurred in private would have seeped out into the histories and memoirs.

A Long War but No Timeline

The military leadership repeatedly stated that the war would be long—a position, which was more perceptive than that held by much of the civilian leadership, who foresaw a short conflict. However, the military leadership never specified what "long" meant, or what the intensity of this long commitment would be. As a result, these statements came off as simple observations, and they lacked the immediacy needed to engage a policy discussion. Dan Bolger notes that the strategic message seemed to be "just give us more time, and our superb fighting forces will eventually produce success."[84]

---

83. Richard B. Myers, *Eyes on the Horizon: Serving on the Front Lines of National Security* (New York: Simon and Schuster), 234.
84. Bolger, *Why We Lost*, xvi.

Table 4: Statements by Senior Military Officers about the Length of the Afghanistan Conflict

Date	Quote	Who
12/22/2001	"It's going to be a long time before these people have the basic necessities for a decent life. We've only made a beginning in this country." [85]	Gen. Franks
2004	"They will have to be crushed. Until that mission is completed, coalition forces will be needed in Afghanistan and Iraq. In September 2001, when I took the operational concept for Afghanistan to the White House for the President's approval, I anticipated that Phase IV could last as long as five years. That was three years ago. From my perspective, we are still on that timeline in Afghanistan." [86]	Gen. Franks
10/3/2006	I think eventually [Afghanistan] will be a success. It just depends on how much time we want to spend doing it."[87]	Gen. James L Jones
10/1/2008	"I think we're still some ways off in all three of those lines of operation—governance, security, and economic reconstruction and development." [88]	Gen. McKiernan
	"I think—first of all, I'm not even looking at an exit strategy right now, but I think as we develop the Afghan army, certainly the enablers like ISR [. . .] have to be in place, so that they have a viable military force when we get to that tipping point we've talked about."	
9/2011	"I think it will take a long time, and we will be training Afghan security forces for perhaps a long time." [89]	Gen. Myers
9/22/2011	"We know that there's got to be something there long-term . . . "[90]	Adm. Mullen
10/8/2015	"If we think that this is going to be cleared up in a couple of years, we're fooling ourselves." [91]	Gen. Campbell
2/19/2019	"The fact of the matter is that we have an enduring interest here to make sure that violent extremist groups in this part of the world can't be used to hurt Americans, American interests and American homeland."[92]	Gen. Votel

Continuing Requests for More Troops

Faced with an expanded mission requiring a political, cultural, and social transformation of Afghanistan, as well as with growing insurgency, the military leadership has continuously asked for more troops. Without question, these requests have been partly driven by the focus on the war in Iraq and the resulting lack of resources available for Afghanistan. Nevertheless, a less ambitious end state would have eliminated the need for more troops in the first place.

---

85. Tommy Franks and Malcolm McConnell, *American Soldier* (New York: HarperCollins Publishers, 2004), 327.
86. Ibid, 550.
87. Jones, *NATO's Role in Afghanistan*.
88. Federal News Service, Inc., "DoD News Briefing with Gen. McKiernan from the Pentagon," news release from October 1, 2008, retrieved from U.S. Department of Defense Archive; Gates, *Memoirs*, 217.
89. "An Interview with Richard B. Myers," *PRISM* 2, no. 4 (September 2011): 151–59.
90. U.S. Senate Committee on Armed Services, *Hearing to Receive Testimony on the U.S. Strategy in Afghanistan and Iraq*, 112th Cong., 1st sess. (2011).
91. Lisa Ferdinando, "Afghanistan at 'Critical Juncture', Campbell Says," U.S. Department of Defense, October 8, 2015.
92. Barbara Starr and Ryan Browne, "US Officials Warn ISIS' Afghan Branch Poses A Major Threat," CNN, February 19, 2019, https://www.cnn.com/2019/02/19/politics/isis-afghanistan-threat/index.html.

Table 5: Statements by Senior Military Officers about the Need for More Troops in Afghanistan

10/1/2008	"Since I got there four months ago, we found we're in a heavier fight, a larger fight in the east, then we had anticipated, so we asked for some immediate forces for Regional Command East with the 101st air assault division. [. . .] to total those up, you could say it was four brigade combat teams with enablers" "What we need is additional military capabilities to provide security for the people in Afghanistan. And until we get to what I call a "tipping point," where the lead for security can be in the hands of the Afghan police, there's going to be a need for the international community to provide military capability."[93]	Gen. McKiernan
8/30/2009	"The campaign in Afghanistan has historically been under-resourced . . . ISAF requires more forces."[94]	Gen. McChrystal
9/4/2009	"It won't work out if we don't" send a lot more [troops].[95]	Gen. Petraeus
6/23/2011	"The ultimate decision was a more aggressive formulation [of withdrawal], if you will, in terms of the timeline, than what we had recommended." [96]	Gen. Petraeus
9/22/2011	"We know that there's got to be something there long-term, but it can't be at that level. So do the Afghans. They understand that."[97] [need something between 2011 and 2018]	Adm. Mullen
7/27/2018	"From my perspective, the decision making on the drawdown was flawed. We came down too fast, and the residual force after December 31, 2014, was too small and on too short a timeline to realistically support the continued development of the Afghan security forces needed to give the Afghans the ability to stand on their feet over the long term." [98]	Gen. Allen

"'We're making real progress,' say last 17 commanders in Afghanistan"

—Duffel Blog

Repeated Statements about Progress

Despite statements about the conflict being long and the need for more troops, the military leadership has continuously stated that it is making progress. This optimism is not surprising given the military's can-do attitude and the human tendency to believe that our efforts will have effect. Nevertheless, when placed against the current state of stalemate, these statements look overly optimistic at best and delusional at worst. Indeed, the statements have been parodied in venues such as *Duffel Blog*.[99]

93. Federal News Service, Inc., "DoD News Briefing with Gen. McKiernan from the Pentagon," news release from October 1, 2008, retrieved from. U.S. Department of Defense Archive.
94. Stanley A. McChrystal, "COMISAF Initial Assessment (Unclassified)," *Washington Post*, Accessed September 21, 2009. https://media.washingtonpost.com/wp-srv/politics/documents/Assessment_Redacted_092109.pdf?sid=ST2009092003140.
95. Gates, *Memoirs*, 367.
96. Scott Wilson, "Mullen, Petraeus Back Obama's Afghanistan Drawdown Plan, Acknowledge Risks," *Washington Post*, June 23, 2011.
97. U.S. Senate Committee on Armed Services, *Hearing to Receive Testimony on the U.S. Strategy in Afghanistan and Iraq*, 112th Cong., 1st sess. (2011).
98. Michael Miklaucic, "Interview with General John R. Allen, USMC (ret.)," PRISM 7, no. 4 (July 27, 2018): 148-54.
99. Text box quotation from "Cat Astronaut," "'We're making real progress,' say last 17 commanders in Afghani-

Several persons interviewed for this study pointed out that these statements might have been intended to sustain the morale of U.S. military forces and the Afghan government, as much as they were meant to illuminate the situation on the ground for decision-makers and the public. Further, the senior civilian leadership has made it clear that military statements should not contradict administration policy. Nevertheless, regardless of their motivation, these statements are the public positions of the military leadership.

Table 5: Statements by Senior Military Officers about Progress in Afghanistan

Date	Quote	Who?
12/19/2001	"We've killed a lot of Taliban and Al Qaeda, Mr. Secretary. The terrorists are literally heading for the hills, toward their traditional refuges in the Spin Mountains." [100]	Gen. Franks
Feb-2005	"Afghanistan is a place where military and economic, political and diplomatic activity at both the national level of the United States and also the international level came together in a way that, over the three years that we've been operating there, has shown interesting progress." "[T]here has been a tremendous amount of progress, and people are generally very optimistic."[101]	Gen. Abizaid
Mar-2005	Abizaid said he was "optimistic" about future developments in Afghanistan and across the Middle East. "I think 2005 can be a decisive year." [102]	Gen. Abizaid
9/13/2006	"We're not going down the tubes here, and the Taliban does not have the upper hand. We're killing a lot of them, getting to sufficient numbers of their leaders and having great effect. I think we're in pretty good shape when it comes to the Taliban." [103]	Gen. Votel
	"I'm with Dan [McNeill] on the prospects in Afghanistan—it's not as gloomy as some would have you believe." [104]	Adm. Fallon
9/12/2007	"I'd like to point out that there is significant progress in the forward movement of the Afghan National Army." [105]	Gen. McNeill
10/1/2008	"I will tell you that I'm more convinced than ever that the insurgency will not win in Afghanistan." [106]	Gen. McKiernan
7/31/2003	"Through the efforts of Combined Joint Task Force 180 [coalition forces in Afghanistan], the stability of Afghanistan grows daily."[107]	Gen. Myers

stan," Duffel Blog, February 27, 2017, https://www.duffelblog.com/2017/02/were-making-real-progress-say-last-17-commanders-in-Afghanistan/.

100. Franks and McConnell, *American Soldier*, 345.

101. John Valceanu, "Abizaid Discusses Progress in Afghanistan," Armed Forces Press Service, February 20, 2005, https://archive.defense.gov/news/newsarticle.aspx?id=25847.

102. Gerry J. Gilmore, "Abizaid: 2005 Can Be a Decisive Year Against Extremism," American Forces Press Service, March 2, 2005, https://archive.defense.gov/news/newsarticle.aspx?id=31299.

103. Gates, *Memoirs*, 211.

104. Ibid.

105. Dan McNeill, "Joint Press Conference with General Dan McNeill, Commander of the NATO-led International Security Assistance Force (ISAF) in Afghanistan, and Ambassador Daan Everts, NATO Senior Civilian Representative." NATO. September 12, 2007. Accessed May 15, 2019.

106. Federal News Service, Inc., "DoD News Briefing with Gen. McKiernan from the Pentagon," news release from October 1, 2008, retrieved from. U.S. Department of Defense Archive

107. Staff Sgt. Richard Thompson, "Myers Visits Bagram Air Base," U.S. Department of Defense, July 31, 2003.

3/19/2008	"The alliances made significant progress in the country."[108]	LTG Eikenberry
2008	"Some places have governance, others have prosperity, and some have security, but few have all three. We are winning slower in some places than others." [109]	Gen. McKiernan
3/18/2009	"[The operation in Afghanistan] is absolutely winnable and will be won." [110]	Gen. McKiernan
2/4/2010	"The situation is serious, but I think we have made significant progress in setting conditions in 2009, and beginning some progress, and that we'll make real progress in 2010." [111]	Gen. McChrystal
July-2010	"In the face of an enemy willing to carry out the most barbaric of attacks, progress has been achieved in some critical areas, and we are poised to realize more." [112]	Gen. Petraeus
May-2011	"I really do think that as people look back and see 2010 as the year in Afghanistan . . . that was a turning point." [113]	Gen. Campbell
9/22/2011	"In Afghanistan, I believe the security situation is steadily improving." [114]	Adm. Mullen
2/10/2013	"I think we are on the road to winning."[115]	Gen. Allen
6/12/2013	"At this point, we have made significant progress, but we are not yet at the point where it is completely sustainable." [116]	Gen. Dunford
5/2/2014	"That election seems to be a turning point in the confidence of the [Afghan Security Forces]." [117]	Gen. Dempsey
12/28/2014	"[T]rust and a common vision for a stable, secure, and unified Afghanistan fills me with confidence that we'll continue to be successful. The road before us remains challenging, but we will triumph." [118]	Gen. Campbell
7/28/2016	"I would say overall, our mission in Afghanistan is on a positive trajectory." [119]	Gen. Nicholson
11/28/2017	"[A]s president Ghani said, he believes we have turned a corner, and I agree." [120]	Gen. Nicholson
8/22/2018	"[W]e are seeing the progress towards reconciliation and a peace process that we have never seen before." [121]	Gen. Nicholson

108. Sgt. Brandon Aird, "NATO Progress in Afghanistan Significant, General Says," U.S. Central Command, March 19, 2008.
109. Gates, *Memoirs*, 217.
110. Donna Miles, "General: War in Afghanistan 'Absolutely Winnable'," U.S. Central Command, March 18, 2009.
111. U.S. Senate Committee on Armed Services, *Hearing to Consider the Nomination Of: Lieutenant General Austin S. Miller, USA to Be General and Commander, Resolute and Support Mission, North Atlantic Treaty Organization/Commander, United States Forces-Afghanistan*, 115th Cong., 2nd sess. (2018),18-55.
112. David Gura, "In Letter To ISAF, Gen. David Petraeus Outlines Agenda In Afghanistan," NPR, July 7, 2010.
113. U.S. Senate Committee on Armed Services, *Hearing to Consider the Nomination Of: Lieutenant General Austin S. Miller, USA to Be General and Commander, Resolute and Support Mission, North Atlantic Treaty Organization/Commander, United States Forces-Afghanistan*, 116th Cong., 1st sess. (2019), 18-55.
114. U.S. Senate Committee on Armed Service. *Hearing to Receive Testimony on the U.S. Strategy in Afghanistan and Iraq*, 112th Cong., 1st sess. (September 22, 2011).
115. "Afghan ISAF Commander John Allen Sees 'Road to Winning'," BBC News, February 10, 2013.
116. "US General Dunford: 'Fight for Afghan Rights Not Over'" BBC News, June 12, 2013.
117. Jim Garamone, "Dempsey Calls Election 'Turning Point' for Afghan Forces," United States Department of Defense, May 2, 2014, https://archive.defense.gov/news/newsarticle.aspx?id=122172.
118. "Transition Ceremony Kicks off Resolute Support Mission," NATO, December 28, 2014.
119. "Department of Defense Press Briefing by General Nicholson via Teleconf," U.S. Department of Defense, July 28, 2016.
120. "Department of Defense Press Briefing by General Nicholson via Teleconf," U.S. Department of Defense, November 28, 2017.
121. Ibid.

5 | Superpower Hubris

This Time Will Be Different

This section seeks to understand why the mission expanded without the senior military officers warning about the consequences. It describes several factors that shaped senior military advice, particularly those that impaired judgment about the duration and intensity of the conflict. The section is written with some humility, looking back at history and noting cases where others might have done better than us. As Margaret Thatcher acidly noted, “The wisdom of hindsight, so useful to historians and indeed to authors of memoirs, is sadly denied to practicing politicians.”[122] Nevertheless, this effort must be made, because without a backward view today’s decision-makers have few guideposts about the consequences of their actions.

The central theme here is hubris. The end of the Cold War seemed to imply that everything was possible; overwhelming U.S. military superiority in the regional conflicts that followed reinforced this perception. This environment engendered a measure of hubris. As an earlier CSIS study noted:

> Running through the entire discussion of U.S. attitudes and doctrine about [contemporary] conflict is an extraordinary level of hubris—the overweening pride of Greek tragic heroes from Oedipus to Icarus. Decades of having overwhelming military capabilities and obtaining easy victories over weak adversaries have given the United States an inflated opinion of how good its military is. Senior officials have repeatedly made claims that the U.S. military is not just the best in the world but the best the world has ever known. As with Greek heroes of legend and literature, hubris can lead to downfall.[123]

U.S. military and senior civilian officials believed that the constraints that others had experienced would not apply to the world’s only superpower. Unfortunately, this belief was tragically mistaken.

---

122. Margaret Thatcher, *The Downing Street Years* (New York: Harper Collins, 1993).
123. Mark Cancian, *Coping with Surprise in Great Power Conflicts* (Washington, DC: CSIS, 2018), 6, https://www.csis.org/analysis/coping-surprise-great-power-conflicts.

"Oh, would some power the vision give us, to see ourselves as others see us! It would from many a blunder free us and from foolish notions."

—Robert Burns

Ignoring How Others May See Us

There is a long history of the United States believing in its exceptionalism and its special place in history. This belief is not misplaced: the United States is exceptional. It created a representative government at a time when monarchs and authoritarian regimes ruled the vast majority of people; it welcomed people from all over the world and welded them into a single political entity; and it grew from a small, fragile country on the edge of a wilderness into the world's only superpower.[124]

The United States can also lay claim to many benign activities over the centuries. For example, it rebuilt Europe after the Second World War, and it was instrumental in constructing and maintaining a liberal order that has allowed unprecedented global prosperity and peace among major powers. Nevertheless, the fact of this exceptionalism does not mean that its values have been universally applied when dealing with other countries. Indeed, modern scholarship has been very harsh about U.S. colonial activities in this regard.[125]

Furthermore, others might not accept our values. This discussion was particularly pointed during the 2000s, becoming intertwined with criticism of the "neoconservatives" and the failing Iraq war. Neoconservatives had seen the march towards market economies and representative democracy as unstoppable after the Cold War, and they had urged the United States to use its power to hasten this movement. Failures in the Iraq and Afghanistan wars raised doubts—indeed, opposition—to this view.

Ignoring the Soviet Experience

The U.S. military was aware of the Soviet experience going into the conflict in Afghanistan. How could it not be, since U.S. support of the Afghan opposition to Soviet forces was considered a great Cold War triumph and an important element in the collapse of the Soviet Union? However, the Soviet experience was viewed as irrelevant. Gen. Myers argued that, whereas the United States overran Afghanistan in 2001 with "a few thousand American and Allied special operations forces," "the Soviet Union had tried to pacify Afghanistan with hundreds of thousands of troops—and their effort had ended in failure."[126] Gen. McChrystal further dismissed the Soviet experience, arguing that "the Soviet failure tended to make their actions a cautionary tale rather than a roadmap for us."[127] A comprehensive volume on lessons learned, produced by the National Defense University, does not even mention the Soviets.[128]

---

124. Robert Burns quotation from "To a Louse," 1786.
125. For a recent critique of U.S. overseas conduct, see: Daniel Immerwahr, *How to Hide an Empire: The History of the Greater United States* (Farrar, Straus, and Giroux, 2019).
126. Richard B. Myers, *Eyes on the Horizon: Serving on the Front Lines of National Security* (New York: Simon and Schuster, 2009), 195.
127. McChrystal, *My Share of the Task*, 331.
128. Richard Hooker and Joseph Collins, eds, *Lessons Encountered: Learning from Long War* (Washington DC: National Defense University,2015).

This happened because U.S. analysts viewed the differences between the Soviet and the coalition occupations as fundamental:

- They were invaders, whereas we were liberators;
- They brought an alien communist ideology, whereas we brought universal values; and
- They were extraordinarily violent, whereas we went to great lengths to protect civilians.

None of these beliefs were necessarily wrong. Many Afghans suffered under the Taliban; Western values have been adopted broadly around the world because they are popular, while Communism has virtually disappeared. The Soviets killed thousands of Afghans and drove millions into exile, whereas during the coalition's occupation, many exiles came home.

Although these comparisons were convincing to a Western audience, they did not consider how the U.S. and its coalition looked to the average Afghan. As Gregory Feifer noted in his history of the Soviet war in Afghanistan, to the Afghans, the Americans and the Soviets looked very much alike. Both were infidels, came from far away, had alien manners, and spoke an alien language. Both brought modern weapons of war. Both sought to change the culture in ways that conservative Afghans found objectionable. Not surprisingly, therefore, both faced an insurgency that was often led by the same people.

During their 10-year war in Afghanistan, the Soviets learned many lessons about dealing with the Afghan terrain and people. They had expected a short occupation but became bogged down for a decade. They had immense firepower but had a hard time bringing it to bear against elusive insurgents. They had expected strong local political support but found that leadership was weak and divided. They worked to build up Afghan security forces but faced illiteracy, indifference, and massive desertions. The United States might have learned from this; instead, it ignored the Soviet experience and had to learn all the same lessons on its own.

One story suffices to draw a clear picture:

> Valery Vostrotim, former commander of the Soviet 345th Regiment in Afghanistan, attended a NATO briefing about wartime experiences. One NATO officer instructed the Russian participants about the importance of respecting Muslim customs during house searches. Don't hold your rifle in attack position, he advised, or go barging into women's quarters. Vostrotim stifled an anguished chuckle—he'd known that 20 years earlier.[129]

Ignoring the History of Occupations

A large body of literature has grown up examining the nature of insurgencies and trying to understand what drives their length and intensity. Much of this arose in the 1990s, in response to the occupations of Bosnia, Kosovo, and Somalia. These studies recognized the difficulties and long-term duration of such occupations. As James T. Quinlivan of RAND noted at the time: "[In stability operations] American forces can face substantial and long-term commitments . . . Troops may face repeated deployments to combat-like tours

129. Gregory Feifer, *The Great Gamble: The Soviet War in Afghanistan*, (New York: HarperCollins Publishers, 2009), 285.

for what appeared to be less-than-vital national interests. The effect on retention and ultimately the professional of the force seem likely to be adverse."[130]

An even larger corpus of work arose during the 2000s as a result of the U.S. experience in Iraq and Afghanistan. For example, just as the war in Iraq was about to begin, a RAND study gained prominence because of its mention during a congressional hearing by General Eric Shinseki, then Army Chief of Staff.[131] For that study, Ambassador James Dobbins had led a team that examined seven case studies of occupation—Germany, Japan, Somalia, Haiti, Bosnia, Kosovo, and Afghanistan. The team concluded that:

- Successful nation-building required a high level of effort measured in time, manpower, and money;
- Force density needed to be about 15 security force members for every thousand inhabitants (the rate per thousand at the beginning of the Afghanistan occupation was 0.2);
- There was no quick route to nation-building—five years seems to be the minimum, and some efforts went on for decades; and
- No post-conflict program of reconstruction could turn Somalia, Haiti, or Afghanistan into thriving centers of prosperity.[132]

There was also a literature about the effect of foreign occupations on indigenous populations. David Kilcullen, for example, wrote a widely cited book, *The Accidental Guerrilla*, that examined recent activity in several theaters: Afghanistan (2006-2008), Iraq (2006-2007), East Timor (1999-2000), southern Thailand (2004-2007), and the Federally Administrated Tribal Areas of Pakistan (2006-2008). He concluded that the mere presence of foreigners engendered resistance, irrespective of the reasons for the occupation: "Local people begin to become accidental guerillas . . . because they oppose outside interference in their affairs, because they are rallied to support local tribal or community interests, or because they are alienated by heavy-handed actions of intervening force." He also noted that the resistance included "cultural protectionism" engendered by "perceived U.S. cultural imperialism."[133]

Finally, U.S. citizens in occupied areas tend to talk with urban elites who share their values. These elites are often foreign-educated and speak English, making it easy to interact with them. Getting outside the capital and the urban centers is difficult for reasons of language, security, and comfort. Further, foreign diplomats cannot always choose who they talk to but are constrained by the host country; the problem is that this focus on urban elites ignores the population in the countryside, which often makes up the bulk of the insurgency. It also misleads diplomats and visitors into believing that the westernized attitudes of the urban elites reflect the country at large.

---

130. James T. Quinlivan, "Force Requirements in Stability Operations," *Parameters* (Winter 1995): 59–69.
131. Eric Schmitt, "Army Chief Raises Estimate of G.I.'s Needed in Postwar Iraq," *New York Times*, February 25, 2003, https://www.nytimes.com/2003/02/25/international/middleeast/army-chief-raises-estimate-of-gis-needed-in-postwar.html.
132. James Dobbins et al., *America's Role in Nation-building: from Germany to Iraq* (RAND, 2003).
133. David Kilcullen, *The Accidental Guerrilla: Fighting Small Wars in the Midst of a Big One* (Oxford: Oxford University Press, 2009), 38, 39.

Ignoring the History of Afghanistan

> *When you're wounded and left on Afghanistan's plains,*
> *And the women come out to cut up what remains,*
> *Jest roll to your rifle and blow out your brains*
> *An' go to your Gawd like a soldier.*
>
> *—Rudyard Kipling, The Young British Soldier*

The British like to say that the Soviets invaded Afghanistan only because they had never read Rudyard Kipling's tales of betrayal and suffering in Afghanistan a century earlier.[134] Even a cursory reading of Afghan history shows that Afghanistan may be easy to conquer but is difficult to subdue; for example, the British famously conquered Afghanistan in 1838, but were driven out in 1842, whereupon their column was annihilated save for one single survivor. Similarly, the Mughals conquered the country in the seventeenth century, but subsequently endured a long insurgency led by the celebrated Afghan chieftain Khan Khattak. Other invaders have had similar experiences.

These difficulties all arose from the same enduring phenomenon: although the Afghans are technologically backward and lack the national institutions to field an effective army, they turn these weaknesses into strengths when they resist the rule of outsiders and conduct local insurgencies. As Said Jawad, the Afghan ambassador to the United States, put it: "Afghanistan is a strong nation but a weak state."[135]

Afghans are also infamous for their shifting loyalties. The Western notion of "us versus them" is inapplicable in a culture where loyalties are tribal rather than national or ideological. Thus, General Rashid Dostum, commander of Uzbek forces in Afghanistan, has switched allegiances at least eight times in over 35 years of conflict. He started with a militia allied to the Communists, then turned on the Communists. After that, "he, at one time or another, allied himself with everyone—Masud, Hikmetyar, the Taliban, Masud again—and betrayed everyone with undisguised aplomb. He had also been on every country's payroll receiving funds from Russia, Uzbekistan, Pakistan, Iran, Pakistan, and Turkey."[136] He is still active in Afghan politics.

Ignoring Why the Taliban Fight

In the west, descriptions of the Taliban look like the contemporary equivalent of a medieval morality play. The Taliban are "violent criminals," "brutal," "undereducated tribal thugs," "thugs, criminals, and predators," and "a cruel, barbaric horde."[137] These descriptions are not necessarily untrue—there's a lot of evidence to support them—but

---

134. Feifer, *Gamble*, 6. For Kipling, see, for example, *The Drums of Fore and Aft* (1889), *The Lost Legion* (1892), and especially the last stanza of his poem, *The Young British Soldier*, cited in the text box. Kipling may have been a proponent of Empire, but he was unflinching about the brutality of fighting on the frontier.
135. David Barno, "Fighting 'the Other War ': Counterinsurgency Strategy in Afghanistan, 2003-2005," *Military Review* (September-October 2007): 40.
136. Ahmed Rashid, *Taliban: Militant Islam, Oil and Fundamentalism in Central Asia* (Yale University Press, 2001), 56.
137. Mark Silinsky, *The Taliban: Afghanistan's Most Lethal Insurgents* (Praeger, 2014), 135; Office of the Press Secretary, "Remarks by the President on a New Strategy for Afghanistan and Pakistan; David Forte, "Who is the Taliban?", Heritage Foundation, Sept 26, 2001.; Donald Trump, "Remarks by President Trump on the Strategy in Afghanistan and South Asia," speech presented at Fort Myer, Arlington, Virginia, August 21, 2017.Howard McKeon, "National Press Club Luncheon with Congressman Howard McKeon, "Speech presented at National Press Club, Washington DC, February 24, 2014.

characterizing the Taliban this way makes it hard to take them seriously. Why would anyone join such a movement? Nevertheless, the Taliban have been able to raise an army against the world's most powerful military, and they have kept that army in the field for years despite heavy casualties. Something they represent must resonate with elements of the Afghan population.

A shortfall in the analysis seeking to identify the root cause of the insurgency is that it focuses too heavily on the problems of producing good governance. For example, McChrystal stated: "[the Afghan population] do not trust [the government] to provide their potential needs, such as security, business, and basic services. This crisis of confidence has created fertile ground for the insurgency."[138] Silinsky made a similar point in his study of the Taliban: "the Taliban did not melt away . . . The march towards Western democratic norms did not progress fast or smoothly . . . Expectations of better lives were not met."[139]

Although weak governance may create conditions that allow an insurgency to arise, it does not follow that someone would become an insurgent, forsaking home and risking death, because they believed that the Taliban would run the state more efficiently and effectively. The Taliban's record of governance in the 1990s was abysmal, with ministries run by ideologues, an obsession with religious observation, and a disdain for the public.[140] Something other than "better governance" has to be motivating their recruits.

The reasons why the Taliban fight are many and complex, with experts identifying as motivators Pashtoon disenfranchisement, economic hardship, cultural anxiety, the desire to re-establish community, criminal tendencies, and the need for local security after years of war.[141] However, Seth Jones argues that religious motivations are fundamental: "The Taliban were motivated by a radical interpretation of Sunni Islam derived from Deobandism. The leaders of most other insurgent groups . . . had strong religious motivations to fight."[142]

"What if they just don't want what we want?"

— Ralph Peters

Unfortunately, religion is a blind spot for Western elites and their supporting institutions. This blind spot arises because religion has not been a major driver of conflict in the West since the 1648 Treaty of Westphalia, which ended two centuries of religious strife brought on by the Protestant Reformation.[143] The crusading movement against Islam, so central to the narrative of Islamic extremists, had faded much earlier: the last vestiges of the Crusader Kingdom had disappeared in 1216 with the fall of Acre to the Arabs, and the last Crusade (as they are generally defined) ended in 1254, when Louis IX of France was repulsed in Egypt.

Westerners know intellectually that religion is important, but they ignore how coalition nation-building can feed insurgency by seeming to undermine religious traditions. Our social conventions prevent us from even considering this issue.

---

138. McChrystal, "COMISAF Initial Assessment (Unclassified)," op cit.
139. Silinsky, *The Taliban*, 157–158.
140. For a description of just how bad Taliban governance was, see Rashid, *Taliban: Militant Islam*, ch. 5 "The Taliban in Power."
141. For example, see: Rashid, *Taliban: Militant Islam*, ch. 2 "Kandahar 1994: The Original of the Taliban" and Silinsky, *The Taliban*, ch. 6, "The Taliban's Recovery in Pakistan."
142. Seth Jones, *In the Graveyard of Empires: America's War in Afghanistan* (New York: Norton and Company, 2009), 161.
143. Text box quotation from Ralph Peters, "Getting Counterinsurgency Right," *New York Post*, December 20, 2006.

6 | Should the Military Be Offering Strategic Advice About Goals and End States?

A major constraint on military advice has been hesitation about whether the military should be offering advice on goals and end states at all. Goals and end states are political questions. They belong to the civilian leadership—particularly the president, who is elected by the people of the United States and has the lead role in foreign affairs (though the Congress also has important constitutional responsibilities in this area). For the military to participate in these discussions might erode the line between military and civilian spheres.

In his study of civil-military relations, Eliot Cohen calls this the "normal" view, wherein the civilian leadership determines goals, and the military carries them out.[144] Many military commentators have been attracted to this view because of its implication that the military is superior in strategy implementation: while civilians may set strategic goals, they should not meddle in military operations. Further, it is comfortable. Military officers have spent their careers at the operational and tactical level, and that is where they are comfortable operating, not at the strategic level. The result is what Professor Rosa Brooks termed "the silence of the generals."[145]

This discomfort was evident with General Tommy Franks. In planning for the conflicts in Afghanistan and Iraq, he was uncomfortable considering what would happen after the overthrow of the regime, and, by implication, the political end state of the conflict. As Gen. Myers noted, "I had trouble with Franks on phase IV [post-hostilities operations] planning . . . Despite several phone calls and personal messages to Franks, CENTCOM's planning for phase IV never improved."[146] Since Myers was not in the chain of command,

144. Eliot Cohen, *Supreme Command: Soldiers, Statesmen, and Leadership in Wartime* (New York: the Free Press, 2002).
145. Rosa Brooks, "Obama vs the generals," Politico, November 2013.
146. Richard B. Myers, *Eyes on the Horizon: Serving on the Front Lines of National Security* (New York: Simon and Schuster, 2009), 225. This quotation described the planning for Iraq, but the same problem occurred with planning for Afghanistan.

there was nothing more he could do. Franks, in his reluctance to address phase IV, shared the views of many military officers: that what happened in the stability phase, and by implication, the ultimate goals of the operation, were someone else's responsibility. Indeed, the name "post-hostilities operations" itself implied a nonmilitary mission.

However, Cohen has argued that the political and military spheres are inextricably interwoven at the highest echelons. Military decisions have political implications, just as political decisions have military ones. Further, as Linda Robinson of RAND noted, "determining objectives requires input from the military that will inform the president's decision," because presidents rarely know exactly what their objectives are when conflicts begin.[147]

Discussions of end states and goals are an integral part of strategy, which is itself often portrayed by military writers as the linking of ends, ways, and means.[148] To focus solely on ways and means would mean that the military did not fully participate in discussions of strategy, instead leaving it to civilian decision-makers and their staff. However, this runs contrary to generations of military writing that argues the contrary: that the military leadership should participate in strategy discussions.

Joint doctrine notes military-civilian interaction at the highest levels, though it is vague about just how the military participates:

> At the strategic level, a nation often determines the national (or multinational in the case of an alliance or coalition) guidance that addresses strategic objectives in support of strategic end states and develops and uses national resources to achieve them. The President, aided by the National Security Council, establishes policy and national strategic objectives . . . The Secretary of Defense translates these into strategic military objectives that facilitate identification of the military end state and theater-strategic planning by the combatant commanders (CCDRs). CCDRs usually participate in strategic discussions with the President and Secretary of Defense through the Chairman of the Joint Chiefs of Staff (CJCS) and with partner nations.[149]

Taking military leadership out of the discussion about goals and end states would also undermine one intent of Goldwater Nichols legislation, which was to offer the civilian leadership better strategic advice. The legislation specifically includes the chairman in strategic discussions and makes provisions for the service chiefs and combatant commanders to participate. For example:

> The Chairman of the Joint Chiefs of Staff shall be responsible for the following:
>
> (1) STRATEGIC DIRECTION—Assisting the President and the Secretary of Defense in providing for the strategic direction of the armed forces. "

147. Linda Robinson et al., *Improving Strategic Competence: Lessons from 13 Years of War* (RAND, 2014), 46.
148. Col. Lykke wrote the original construct of "ends, ways, means," which has been picked up widely in military writing, though not without criticism. See: Colonel Arthur Lykke, "Defining Military Strategy," *Military Review* LXIX, no. 5 (1989); for an example in joint doctrine, see JP 5-0 *Joint Planning*, p. I-5.
149. Joint Chiefs of Staff, JP 1 *Doctrine for the Armed Forces of the United States* (2017), https://www.jcs.mil/Portals/36/Documents/Doctrine/pubs/jp1_ch1.pdf.

(2) STRATEGIC PLANNING—Preparing strategic plans, including plans, which conform with resource levels projected by the Secretary of Defense to be available for the period of time for which the plans are to be effective.[150]

Finally, making this connection would encourage accountability. Some military commentators blame battlefield failures on civilian leadership (which certainly deserves criticism), exonerating the military leadership because they see strategy as a civilian responsibility. A classic statement here is that of retired USMC General Joseph Hoar in the context of Vietnam: "The U.S. military forces fought with competence and valor. We were asked to do the unachievable—win a counterinsurgency campaign that could only be won at the end of the day through political means."[151] While this shifting of blame may be comforting, the implied lack of accountability for strategy is harmful in the long run, since military personnel bear the brunt of bad strategic decisions.

Thus, this project concludes that senior military officers owe the president and civilian leadership their best advice about the connection between goals and resources, recognizing that both are variables. What follows are recommendations about how to do this better in the future so that the United States does not blunder into "forever wars."

---

150. *Goldwater-Nichols Department of Defense Reorganization Act of 1986*, Public Law 99-433 (October 1, 1986), https://history.defense.gov/Portals/70/Documents/dod_reforms/Goldwater-NicholsDoDReordAct1986.pdf.
151. Gen. Joseph P. Hoar, USMC (Ret.), "A Marine's Reflections on the End of the Vietnam War," *U.S. Naval Institute*, April 30, 2015, https://news.usni.org/2015/04/30/a-marines-reflections-on-the-end-of-the-vietnam-war.

7 | Recommendations

Eyes Wide Open

The purpose of these recommendations is to help create conditions so that when the United States faces decisions about long-term occupations in the future, it goes into the commitments with its eyes wide open—that is, it understands the choices that it has about end states, as well as the potential length and intensity of the commitment associated with those choices. The United States should not back into such wars—long, expensive, and indecisive—through a combination of good intentions, "can-do spirit," and hubris.

The purpose of these recommendations is not to argue for or against a particular political goal. If future presidents wish to embark on long-term occupation and nation-building, that is the choice that they are authorized to make. They are elected by the U.S. public to make such decisions, and the senior military leadership is not. As noted earlier, the United States has conducted long-term nation-building in the past with great success (although other attempts have ended in failure and tragedy).

Insightful strategic military advice about ends, ways, and means is one element in better decisionmaking. It is certainly not the only element, but it is particularly important for the military, who will have to specify and publicly defend the forces and military effort required for a given conflict, and then to implement the strategy on the ground.

Create a Dialogue Between Senior Military and Civilian Leaders About Goals and End States

Creating a dialogue about end states is one of those think tank recommendations that makes a lot of sense and rolls easily out of the word processor but is, in fact, extremely hard to accomplish in real life. The reason is twofold. First, many senior civilian leaders have strong opinions that discourage dialogue. For example, in 2003, when Gen. Shinseki offered the opinion that the occupation of Iraq would require large forces, he was publicly slapped down. Other senior leaders got the message.[152] Gen. McChrystal's 2010 firing,

152. Eric Schmitt, "Pentagon Contradicts General on Iraq Occupation Force Size," *New York Times*, February 28, 2003, https://www.nytimes.com/2003/02/28/us/threats-responses-military-spending-pentagon-contradicts-gen-

which happened after his staff over-shared with a journalist, seemed to reinforce the point about being cautious in expressing opinions.

Second, civilians and the military approach the problem differently. As General Martin Dempsey noted, "if you are an elected official, the likelihood of your conceiving a well-crafted and well-defined objective at the beginning is almost zero . . . Elected officials are hardwired to ask for options first and then reverse engineer objectives. The military is hardwired to do exactly the opposite."[153]

Nevertheless, this kind of discussion is important because it is fundamental to the direction and ultimate success of the conflict. As Frank Hoffman, a noted Washington strategist, lamented: "The need to think strategically about the ends/ways/means chain is quite evident in the conduct of strategy in Iraq and Afghanistan. What was generally lacking or astrategic about U.S. actions was the lack of a coherent linkage between desired ends and the ultimate means required. Failures in council to create a strategic logic and coherent linkages that bound the application of military, diplomatic, and developmental resources to the desired strategic effect. Thanks to bureaucratic blinders and personal blind spots inside the National Security Council and at the theater command, American strategists have frequently struggled with preserving a logic chain in recent conflicts."[154]

Eliot Cohen pointed to a solution even though he was coming at it from the angle of civilian leaders. He noted that the relationship between civilian leaders and senior military officers was "an unequaled dialogue," since the civilian leaders held ultimate power. Nevertheless, successful civilian leaders did not "dictate to their [military] subordinates," rather "the practice of these men was interaction." He describes how probing questions from the civilians and the resulting discussions with military officers elicited assumptions and implications that had not been clear before. From this, a better decision could be made.[155]

To encourage discussion and avoid the criticism from civilian leaders with fixed opinions, the military might use "if . . . then" statements. Rather than say "nation-building in Afghanistan will not succeed," a senior military officer might say, "nation-building in Afghanistan may succeed if the United States commits to having advisory and support forces there for several decades." Gen. Dempsey made this point: "if you want me to do X, here is what I think I need to do. If you think I need to do it for less, then I'm going to do less . . . We will not ask a brigade to do a division's worth of work."[156]

Despite Gen. Dempsey's admonition, military officers are inclined to a "can-do" attitude when faced with a tough challenge. This is admirable and generally desirable, but not when it disguises, or leaves undiscussed, the true costs of achieving the civilians' goals.

---

eral-iraq-occupation.html. To be fair to the political leadership, the congressional hearing was the first they heard of Shinseki's concerns, so they were taken by surprise.

153. Dempsey, quoted in Hooker and Collins, *From the Chairman*.

154. Frank Hoffman, "Considerations in Grand Strategy," *Orbis* (Summer 2014).

155. Cohen, *Supreme Command*, 208, 209.

156. Dempsey, quoted in Hooker and Collins, *From the Chairman*.

Potential mechanisms for achieving this dialogue are many—NSC working groups, deputies' committees, personal relationships, and outside consultants—and go beyond the scope of this paper. The key point, however, is that mechanisms are available to fit the personality and decisionmaking style of the president and secretary of defense.

Require More Clarity from Civilian Officials

UPDATE AUMFS

Updating Authorizations for the Use of Military Force (AUMFs) might act as a mechanism to force a dialogue between senior civilian officials and military officials about the goals and end states for military campaigns and the length and intensity of the commitment. Currently, U.S. military forces are conducting a wide variety of global operations under vague AUMFs from 2001 and 2002. Efforts to update AUMFs to align more closely to current operations have failed, as every proposal engenders some opposition. Vagueness pleases few but seems to be the default position.

Constructing and then legislating AUMFs is, of course, difficult to do, but it would be an excellent tool for encouraging dialogue. It would also improve the accountability of the executive branch and enhance the moribund role of Congress in deciding issues of war and peace.

"We need strategists. In the Army and across the services. At all levels. We need senior generals and admirals who can provide solid military advice to our political leadership, and we need young officers who can provide solid military advice—options, details, the results of analysis—to the generals and admirals....We need young strategists because we need senior strategists, and we need a lot because when the time comes we need enough."

— General John R. Galvin
then-supreme allied commander, Europe (SACEUR)

Continue to Develop Military Strategists

There has long been a belief that the post-Cold War U.S. military is tactically and technically proficient but strategically inept.[157] As a result, the military services have made an effort to improve their strategic thinking by creating special programs to train strategists, with the Army's program being the most well-developed. As described in an earlier CSIS study on strategy formulation: "Three decades [after General Galvin's article] DoD has made some progress toward answering General Galvin's call for professionals who practice strategic thinking. Nevertheless, Congress and others remain concerned that the formulation of good strategy is inhibited by the lack of qualified strategists." [158] The CSIS study described what the services are doing and additional steps that they might take to develop a cadre of military strategists.[159]

157. For example, see: Jason Warren, "The Centurion Mind Set in the Army's Strategic Leader Paradigm," *Parameters* (summer 2015): 35-46.
158. Quotation in text box from John R. Galvin, "What's the Matter with Being a Strategist?" *Parameters*, 19 (March 1989): 2, 4.
159. Mark Cancian et al., *Formulating National Security Strategy: Past Experience and Future Choices* (Washington, DC: CSIS, 2017), https://www.csis.org/analysis/formulating-national-security-strategy.

The particular value of strategists in this context—creating coherence between ends, ways, and means—is that they are more inclined to ask fundamental questions: Who is the enemy? What constitutes success?[160] Facing these questions may, in turn, avoid the Harry Summers lament of a U.S. military winning all the battles but losing the war.[161]

The greater challenge is not in developing strategists but in developing strategists who are credible to senior military leaders (at the three and four-star level). Concurrently, there is a need for senior military leaders to be willing to use the insight of strategists in their dealings with civilian decision-makers at the highest levels.

To be blunt, the senior military leadership needs to have enough confidence in the advice it is getting from strategists to tell civilian leadership: "We can build an Afghanistan with a representative government, a market economy, a centralized and efficient bureaucracy, empowered women and girls, and tolerant of all religions, but it will take two generations. Are you willing to make that commitment?"

The subject of strategic education for military offices goes beyond the scope of this study. However, two approaches seem important. First, education in strategy should continue to be conducted at the top-level military schools. This will ensure that the military officers most likely to rise to senior positions will have some exposure to the concepts of strategy, as well as an understanding of how those differ from the tactical and operational challenges they have previously faced in their careers. This will not turn all officers into strategists, nor should it, but it may make senior leaders more open to listening to strategists' advice.

Second, strategists should be made credible to the senior warfighting leadership. All the service programs for developing strategists already do this to some degree, mixing strategic training and experience in traditional military operations, but it is particularly important because senior leaders need to regard strategists as providing credible advice in a warfighting situation. If senior leaders want purely academic strategic advice, they can bring on civilian strategists; military strategists need to bridge both worlds. They should not be regarded as outsiders who are smart and well-educated but not relevant to the decisions that warfighters must make.

Take Seriously the History and Experience of Others

Historians have argued that history can inform strategy ever since Thucydides dissected the Peloponnesian wars. Such sentiments have been picked up by military officers through the ages. For example, Gen. Douglas MacArthur said: "More than most professions, the military is forced to depend on intelligent interpretation of the past for signposts charting the future. Devoid of opportunity in peace for self-instruction through actual practice of his profession, the soldier makes maximum use of the historical record in assuring the readiness of himself and his command to function efficiently in an emergency."[162] A serious study of history might help avoid the various "ignorances" described in Chapter 5.

160. For an excellent discussion of the distinction between "victory," which implies a maximalist outcome, and "success," which allows for something less, see Robinson et al., *Strategic Competence*, 99.
161. Harry G. Summers, *On Strategy: A Critical Analysis of the Vietnam War* (Presidio Press, 1982).
162. Michael Evans, "A Usable Past: A Contemporary Approach to History for the Western Profession of Arms," *Defense and Security Analysis*, Vol. 35(2019).

There is a continuing struggle with "presentism," the notion that the present time is unique and therefore beyond the reach of historical insight. Thus, Williamson Murray and Richard Hart Sinnreich complain about an "unacknowledged conviction of too many of those responsible for national security decisions, civilian and military, that history has little to offer today's defense policymaker."[163]

Part of the problem is that civilian universities are not producing historians, particularly military historians. The study of history has declined precipitously in the last several decades, and what remains is typically focused on issues of identity that resonate in the academy. Although military history remains highly popular with the public, few professional historians are available to teach in the military education system.[164] Fortunately, a movement has arisen to challenge this trend and to encourage the use of history in public policy. The movement is broad, with projects as diverse as the Applied History Project at Harvard's Kennedy School of Government and the CSIS program on military and diplomatic history.[165]

The present report adds its voice about the need for a deeper understanding and application of history in the military profession. This can open the aperture of possibilities that decisionmakers and their staff consider, as well as mitigate the inevitable effects of superpower hubris by reminding practitioners of the challenges and opportunities that arose in analogous situations in the past.

Revise Doctrine Manuals to Include a Discussion of End States

The selection of end states and goals matters to military organizations because they achieve these on the ground. Yet, as noted earlier, FM 3-24 does not link the choice of strategic goals and end states to the length, intensity, and nature of the counterinsurgency fight. An obvious step would be to include such a discussion in the next revision of the manual. The bottom line would be that the deeper the political, social, and cultural transformation being sought in the host country, the longer, broader, and more intense the counterinsurgency campaign will be. Further, this is a choice, not an inevitable consequence of the intervention.

Because FM 3-24 is a "field" manual, that discussion would likely be brief, noting the connection and discussing its importance but not getting into the details of the strategic decision-making. Other joint publications that cover higher levels of decision-making, for example, JP-3 Operations, should include that discussion in more detail, not only for counterinsurgency but for all conflicts.

---

163. Williamson Murray and Richard Hart Sinnreich, *The Importance of History to the Military Profession* (New York: Cambridge University Press, 2006), 5

164. For a description of this problem, see: Hal Brands and Francis Gavin, "The Historical Profession Is Committing Slow-Motion Suicide," War on the Rocks, December 10, 2018.

165. For information on the Applied History Project, see https://www.belfercenter.org/project/applied-history-project; for information on the CSIS Program on Military and Diplomatic History, see https://www.csis.org/programs/international-security-program/isp-archives/project-military-and-diplomatic-history.

About the Author

Mark F. Cancian (Colonel, USMCR, Ret.) is a senior adviser with the CSIS International Security Program. He joined CSIS in April 2015 from the Office of Management and Budget, where he spent more than seven years as chief of the Force Structure and Investment Division, working on issues such as Department of Defense budget strategy, war funding, and procurement programs, as well as nuclear weapons development and nonproliferation activities in the Department of Energy. Previously, he worked on force structure and acquisition issues in the Office of the Secretary of Defense and ran research and executive programs at Harvard University's Kennedy School of Government. In the military, Colonel Cancian spent over three decades in the U.S. Marine Corps, active and reserve, serving as an infantry, artillery, and civil affairs officer and on overseas tours in Vietnam, Desert Storm, and Iraq (twice). Since 2000, he has been an adjunct faculty member at the Johns Hopkins School of Advanced International Studies, where he teaches a course on the connection between policy and analysis. A prolific author, he has published over 40 articles on military operations, acquisition, budgets, and strategy and received numerous writing awards. He graduated with high honors (magna cum laude) from Harvard College and with highest honors (Baker Scholar) from Harvard Business School.